After a long and satisfying career in the corporate world, how does a successful manager, professional, or executive assure himself or herself a continuation of feeling useful and needed? He or she wins the age game by reading the Ballards' book and keeping it handy for ready reference.

—Rex D. Adams, Vice President of Human Resources
Mobil Corporation

When the youngest of our six children entered school, I began preparing for life-without-children. I am convinced that the launching of a new career or the fostering of neglected interests guarantees "beating the age game"—and the empty nest syndrome. The Ballards offer exciting, yet practical ways to plan for the third half of life. Should be read by all women over 45.

—Ann F. Caron, Ed. D., Psychologist and author

Beating the Age Game: Redefining Retirement is a refreshing and practical guide for those beginning to look seriously at their "Third Age." Well founded in philosophical and psychological insights, it offers strategies not only to cope with but to utilize the gift of this new facet of the human journey. I hope that individuals, couples, and study groups will use it as a starting point for the reflection and decision making which are essential if this period is to be one of grace and growth rather than decline and decay.

—Msgr. Charles J. Fahey, Third Age Center
Fordham University

The Ballards have added an important book to the growing body of literature that is redefining retirement in America. This upbeat look at the many facets of post-career life will start you down the pathway to freedom where you will find fulfillment in the third half of your life.

—M. Elvin Haynes, President
International Society for Retirement Planning

Our communities need all the help they can get from experienced, competent people. Every business person concerned about how to enjoy the rest of life to the fullest will find the how and the why in this book, which recognizes that retirement offers the best "commencement" since college.

—Arthur M. McCully, President
National Executive Service Corps

Twenty or more years to do precisely what *you* want to do. What an opportunity! No notion of what it is you want to do and not a clue as to how to discover it. What a tragedy! In *Beating the Age Game,* Jack and Phoebe Ballard provide everyone who is planning to retire an inspiring, informative and practical guide to seizing the opportunity, avoiding the tragedy, and leading richer, longer, more rewarding lives.

—Carl S. Sloane, Professor
Harvard Business School

In *Beating the Age Game: Redefining Retirement,* the Ballards have created, finally, a really meaningful approach to living and thriving after the long years of service to the organization. The real brillance in the book is that it prescribes not only the practical aspects of living your life after retiring, but does the much more important job of transforming the whole purpose of "life after Work." The book is empowering, exciting to read, and a significant contribution to men and women of all ages dealing with the issues of structuring and managing their own lives. Hurrah!

—Gerald M Sturman, Chairman
The Career Development Team, Inc.

The Ballards are doing the world a big favor with *Beating the Age Game.*
The poet Robert Browning wrote, "Grow old along with me/The best is still to be/The last of life, for which the first was made." As the above–65 portion of America's population increases, it becomes evermore important to make those extra years a time—as Browning indicated—of quality and growth. But there aren't a lot of instructions on how to grow old happily. *Beating the Age Game* helps to fill that gap. It offers sound, sensible and personally fulfilling advice, which is good for both the individual and society.

—John W. White, Literary agent and author

BEATING THE AGE GAME

JACK & PHOEBE BALLARD

BEATING THE AGE GAME

REDEFINING RETIREMENT

MASTERMEDIA LIMITED · NEW YORK

This book is dedicated to:

The memory of Bob and Esther Greenleaf, who first introduced us to the higher concepts of Carl Rogers and Carl Jung, and to the continuing search for personal growth.

The memory of Woodrow Wilson, whose articulation of the idea of being in the nation's service helped join us in our "first half," has motivated us throughout our "second half," and will continue to stretch us in our "third half."

Jan, our eldest son, who first urged us to write this book, and who is dedicating his life to being in the nation's service.

Copyright © 1993 Jack and Phoebe Ballard

All rights reserved, including the right
of reproduction in whole or in part in
any form. Published by MasterMedia Limited.
MASTERMEDIA and colophon are registered
trademarks of MasterMedia Limited.

The *Third Half of Life* is a registered trademark.

Library of Congress Cataloging-in-Publication Data
Ballard, Jack.
    Beating the age game : redefining retirement / Jack & Phoebe
Ballard.
        p. cm.
    Includes bibliographical references.
    ISBN 0-942361-79-2 : $12.95
    1. Retirement—United States—Planning.   2. Aged—United States—
Life skills guides.   I. Ballard, Phoebe.   II. Title.
HQ1063.2.U6B35 1993
646.7'9—dc20   93-19494
                                                                     CIP

Designed by Jacqueline Schuman
Production services by Martin Cook Associates, Ltd., New York
Manufactured in the United States of America.

10 9 8 7 6 5 4 3 2 1

CONTENTS

CONTENTS

ACKNOWLEDGMENTS

We want to express our deepest appreciation to all who gave us encouragement along the way, and without whose unselfish help we would probably be nowhere today.

Shelley Freeman, who believed in it so strongly that she contributed the financial section with no strings attached.

Faith Hamlin, who believed in this book and invested exhaustive efforts to make it happen.

Our editor, Bob Pearson who helped so much to "make the writing sing," Dick Wedemeyer who did an early copy-edit, Joan Warburg who proofed the galleys, and Diana Lynn and Christopher Turek who polished off the whole book.

Bob and Michael Ballard, whose love and support never failed to give us the courage to keep going.

Our parents, whose example has never failed to stand us in good stead.

Tom and Ellie Jackson, who gave us a boost to get started with the Third Half of Life project in the first place.

Jerry and Peggy Bier-Sturman, who have been such a continuing source of support at every stage of the game.

Nancy Low and Susan Abbott, whose interest and professional competence helped launch our initial project.

Our Board of Advisors, who have supported us through thick and thin, and from whom we have all along drawn enormous strength

ACKNOWLEDGMENTS

and support: Jack and Lela Bogardus, Brook Calkin, John and Ann Caron, Ruth Crosby, Mike and Kip Farrell, Bill and Muffie Lynch, Peter and Barbara McSpadden, Ted Robinson, Bill Spencer, Brenda and Tom Stiers, Roy and Connie Welch, Bob Zimmerman.

Ron Conarroe, Kyle and Linda Felt, Oscar and Miriam Lubow, George and Betty McMoran, whose encouragement, valuable feedback, and constructive criticism have contributed so much to the final product.

Sydney Reynolds, who helped us find the way to our wonderful publisher, Susan Stautberg.

And all the others who have been supportive, encouraging, and helpful in endless ways.

PREFACE

NOW WHAT DO I DO?

As a student preparing for a career, this question was foremost in your mind. Now, if you are like most people, you think of post-career planning as something to be done late in your full-time career, in order to ensure financial security when you stop working. This is an unfortunate misconception.

What you should do is life planning, ideally starting in your forties, but no later than your fifties. Your plan should focus on both financial and lifestyle goals. Thinking about your future involves the search for a vision—a vision containing a larger picture of your life, a new perspective about yourself and what you want out of life, and some sense of how to make your future count.

If you are at the midstage of life or beyond, the time will soon come when your family is safely launched, your nest egg is adequately built, and the hard slogging isn't necessary any more. If you have done your homework, you can look forward to the best, and most satisfying time of your life.

Your vision about this stage of life should encompass a balance of leisure time, learning, and some kind of lifework that turns you on. According to a Zen saying, "As the natural medium of a fish is water, and a bird air, the natural medium of a person is work."

When you shift out of your full-time career, you may wish to work

less—and on your own terms—but to loaf is fatal. The early death
rate of traditional retirees proves that. Finally, your vision needs to
include an ultimate meaning for your life. When all is said and done,
what do you want it all to add up to?

Remember your last vacation. Toward the end, weren't you a little
restless and bored, and actually looking forward to getting back to
work? Now try to picture a twenty- to thirty-year vacation. Well, if
you retire in the typical way, say, at age sixty, that's just what you
would get: a twenty- to thirty-year vacation. If that doesn't scare you
into *at least beginning* to think about your future, it should!

This book makes a case *against* the standard practice of retirement
for two reasons: first, it isn't good for *you,* and secondly, it isn't good
for *society.*

WHO SAYS?

We are Jack and Phoebe Ballard, a couple in our sixties, who've been
married forty years, and are heavily involved in life planning. Here's
how it came about.

We had been married about ten years, had two young children,
and had most of the material things we needed. Our initial goals had
been attained. Yet we didn't see any future beyond the cycle of
diapers, bottles, and commuter trains, broken only by the occasional
dinner party or outing. In the words of Peggy Lee, we were asking
ourselves, "Is that all there is?"

The answer began to unfold when we happened onto Wainwright
House, a personal growth center in Rye, New York. There we
came in contact with some philosophical concepts that changed
our lives. We began to realize that continuous growth and development are not only possible, they are, in fact, *the purpose of life.*
All vital human beings are constantly becoming more the person
they are intended to be.

This is not a new idea. The late Norman Cousins characterized it
as "human perfectibility," drawing his ideas from a 1903 book by
Elie Metchnikoff entitled *The Nature of Man: Studies in Optimistic
Philosophy.* Cousins said, "It remained for a Russian to write a book
about the organization and function of the human body that corre-
sponds to the dominant American political and philosophical strain,

beginning with Jefferson, Franklin, and Adams, and extending through Emerson, Fuller, William James, Pierce, and John Dewey. That strain is connected with the idea of human perfectibility. Not perfection, for no one can define the outer reaches of perfection, but perfectibility as represented by creative growth, betterment, and the pursuit of human potentialities."

So we began our own search. Countless books opened our eyes to a new and exciting world. We explored Arnold Toynbee's and Will Durant's interpretations of patterns, meanings, and lessons of history. Through Teilhard de Chardin we got new insights into the Judeo-Christian religion. We became excited by new ideas about the concept of God, beginning with Bishop Robinson's suggestion that He is not "up there with a white beard," but rather an energy for good within us all, readily accessible through prayer and meditation. We devoured books by gurus and mystics such as Gerald Heard, Paul Tillich, Thomas Kelly, and Henri Nouwen.

We discovered an enormous body of knowledge about the union of psychology and religion begun by Carl Jung and continued by Joseph Campbell, Scott Peck, Robert Johnson, and Jack Sanford, among others. They didn't preach that we *should* change and grow. Rather, they gave us the tools for doing it.

We were exposed to Eastern religions through books by William Johnston, D.T. Suzuki, Paramahansa Yogananda and many others, which contributed to our understanding of the universality of "truth." We learned about such ideas as synergy, synchronicity, nonattachment and the validity of "myth." We began to see life as a journey with meaning, in which we were constantly developing and unlocking more potential from within.

As we deepened our appreciation of our spiritual and philosophical heritage, we spent seven years living overseas, first in South America, then Europe. This experience strengthened our appreciation of our American heritage, especially our freedom.

Back in the United States, Jack continued his corporate career and Phoebe became program director of Wainwright House. During this time, she returned to university for a degree and training in psychotherapy.

We settled near our parents and watched them and their friends get older. In many cases, after the men retired to a life of leisure, they soon seemed to wither away and die. Later, we saw the same thing happen to people only a few years older than we. In a single shocking year, we saw the death of *seven* men with whom Jack had worked, yet all were in good health when they had retired only two or three years previously.

Using Jack's corporate experience in management and professional development, and Phoebe's psychotherapy background, we decided to create the "Third Half of Life Seminar." Our goal was to provide people with an opportunity to stand back from their lives and think about themselves, and to build a framework for their future. (See Appendix)

Based on our research and consulting on the subject, as well as our own previous work lives, we see a dramatic phenomenon emerging. This book tells what we see happening and why it makes sense philosophically.

We hope to encourage readers in midlife to begin creating a framework for your future. Start planning now for the time when "school's out" and you're free to fulfill your dreams and expectations. And to those of you who've already reached your sixties, we hope to drive home the point that you don't have to buy into the old notion of retirement. Rather, shift gears. Have more leisure time but also keep learning and doing something productive that you enjoy. And finally, we explain, step by step, how to go about making the next period of your life the best one yet.

WHAT IS SAID?

Five fundamental factors revolutionizing our culture form the key themes in this book:

The New Longevity

Until the end of the nineteenth century, life was divided into two parts: under twenty, you were young; over twenty, you were old. More recently, there seemed to be three divisions: under twenty, you were growing up and being educated; from twenty to fifty, you were raising families and working to gain financial security; and over fifty, you were becoming old and dying.

In the past thirty years, a dramatic change has occurred. Thanks to medical advances and better health habits, especially nutrition and exercise, life can begin again at sixty and extend well into the eighties, nineties, and hundreds. In fact, the latest census reveals there are 35,000 people over one hundred years of age in the United States alone. And not only are we going to live a lot longer, we're going to be more healthy and active as well. Current scientific thinking says that *if* we take proper care of ourselves, we can remain healthy until the day we die. The mythical fountain of youth has been discovered.

The challenge is, what are *you* going to do about it? Many people in their nineties today realize how young they actually were in their sixties and seventies. They are mystified as to why they didn't *think* and *act* as young as they obviously were. They feel they have missed something, but aren't sure they could have done anything differently. The truth is, most could have.

The Need for a "Work"

What they should have done, rather than retire from life, was continue some kind of work. The key to vigor and enjoyment of life at any age is to be challenged, productive, and involved. Only by having a work—projects or activities to which you can dedicate your heart, energy and know-how—can you find real fulfillment.

This work must be directed beyond yourself and your family. To do something for others, while at the same time enjoying the effort, makes all the difference in how you feel about yourself. The work can be unique to you, tapping your own special skills, experience, and dreams.

Meaning and Purpose

Previously, a person's post-career concerns were threefold: money, health, and location. These concerns were self-centered, perhaps with an emphasis on family. Today, a fourth dimension is emerging. Our society is discovering that a *lifework* which satisfies the self and energizes others provides essential meaning and purpose to our lives.

Having a meaning and purpose in life underlies *everything*. Without that key ingredient, life is lukewarm and empty. But your lifework will keep you involved and interested. We all need to be needed. And we need to care.

PREFACE

The "Third Half" of Life

The concept of aging is changing. We know that for most people today, ages forty and fifty involve a lot of hard work, self-discipline, responsibility, and sacrifice. At age fifty-five or sixty, we are just reaching our prime. That is when the real fun can begin. Potentially the best years are still to come.

So in our seminars and in this book, we call the stage between fifty-five and at least eighty the "third half of life." By the word "half" we mean that this period *can* constitute an *extra* half! And it can be the most satisfying and enjoyable "half" of all!

Planning Ahead

To take full advantage of the freedom and flexibility in your third half, you need to plan ahead. You have so many choices and opportunities. Perhaps for the first time in your life, you will find a balance among learning, leisure and work.

Planning ahead embraces two basic considerations: lifestyle and finances. Most of us spend some time on the latter, as a matter of necessity; too few spend enough time, if any, on the former. Yet, without a fulfilling and enjoyable life, what good is all the money in the world?

PEOPLE DOING THEIR OWN THING

If you are like most, the "third half of life" will be your first chance to really "do your own thing." You may opt for a complete change to something for which you have a talent and which you've always wanted to do. Or you might want to continue what you're doing now but change "where" or "how much." Here are some examples of what some others are doing:

- A former sales representative for a major office supply company wanted to make a complete change. Handy with tools and liking to work with his hands, he is using his wood-working skills, and helping to manage a low-cost housing program in a suburban area two days a week.
- An urban policeman took a position that moved him into the wilds where he wanted to be. He became chief of a national park security force with jurisdiction over roads, camping areas, golf

courses and residential and agricultural properties—in short, the variety and kind of environment he hankered for.

· An account executive in advertising also wanted a complete change. In college he had played clarinet in a band. At age fifty-five, he unearthed his beloved clarinet and started his own Dixieland band, which performs regularly, much to his enjoyment and delight. During the day, he and his wife remodel old houses.

· A longtime employee of an insurance company didn't want to work full time anymore. She joined her company's "retiree job bank," filling jobs as needed and as mutually convenient. She enjoys the flexibility and having time for herself and her family. She also loves returning to the office to see her friends and former associates. She likes the extra income and the company appreciates her willingness to help.

· Doctors are making changes in their work life while staying in medicine. Some have closed their practices, but stay involved in local hospitals a few days a week. Others have left their practices to go elsewhere. One such example is an internist who spends two weeks every quarter working in a clinic on a Caribbean island. He charges well below his usual rate because he believes it's important for people to pay something for services received. Another, a surgeon, spends time working in a clinic in Africa.

· A former housewife and mother started training in gourmet cooking after her children grew up. She contracted to manage an inn and function as its chef, with an option to receive part payment in equity. She now owns the place!

· Another woman of the same background and inclination started a successful catering business, specializing in corporate lunches that she takes into company offices for special occasions. She is able to charge fancy prices because the food is so good!

· A businessman with a lifelong yen to be a sculptor, enrolled in a master's degree program after he retired. Today, he's an accomplished sculptor, selling some of his work, and donating other pieces to institutions he cares about. He's also returned to consulting for businesses, which he does when he isn't sculpting. This has given him a satisfying balance in his life.

PREFACE

There are hundreds of such stories and they all add up to excitement—the kind of excitement that goes along with major change and progress. This book attempts to pinpoint that change; to analyze why it's happening; to suggest ways of getting on board and riding it successfully; and to imagine the far-reaching results it could lead to.

Finally, this book is not based on theory or scholarly research. Rather, it reflects observations in our own life together, plus ten years of experience in conducting seminars and consulting. The evidence thus obtained has convinced us beyond a doubt that the years after age fifty-five can indeed be the "golden years." And the good news is that these "golden years" are attainable for anyone who begins planning early enough. If you are in your forties or fifties, you need to start now.

By the year 2000, there will be thirty-four million Americans aged sixty-five and over. Because of the huge baby-boomer population coming along, which Ken Dychtwald describes in his book, *Age-Wave,* as "a rising tide,"—these numbers will double by the year 2050. Dychtwald estimates that by then, one person in four will be over sixty-five. It is awesome to contemplate the far-reaching implications that this new kind of energy could have on our world.

This book is divided into four sections.

Part I: "The New Perspective" provides background and evidence of the timeliness of this cultural revolution.

Part II: "How to Make It Happen" brings the theory down to a practical level and provides a seven-point program that shows exactly how to go about planning your lifestyle.

Part III: "Your Money" gets down to dollars and "sense," offering expert guidance on managing your finances.

Part IV: "A Changing America" suggests the potential power of the sociological change that is taking place.

If you want to beat the age game, now's the time to begin. Reinvent your life and make the "third half" your best and most rewarding years.

—Jack and Phoebe Ballard

THE NEW PERSPECTIVE

In America today, there is a new phenomenon at work, thanks to the new life expectancy. Because of better health habits and modern medicine, people are living longer—often by twenty to thirty years! A quiet cultural revolution that will affect everyone is taking place.

The "silent" generation, people now in their fifties and sixties, is leading the revolt, partly because their children, the "baby boomers," pushed them into it. The most visible manifestation of this revolution is that more and more people are rejecting the traditional model of retirement. Rather than "going out to pasture," they are going after something different and achieving a new quality of life hitherto unavailable.

The new model involves continuing participation, involvement, and productivity. For people over fifty, there is a bright future previously unheard of. But people need to start preparing for it in mid-life—or risk missing out on what could be their best years.

People are now recognizing that the theories of human development apply throughout life—that the purpose of human existence is to continue to mature until the day you die. A new concept of "work" as service to others is emerging, along with the confidence that each of us can continue to contribute and make a difference.

BEATING THE AGE GAME

While you are still involved in your full-time career, start contemplating your long-term future. Is there life after a full-time career? You bet there is! This will be your chance to, as the late Joseph Campbell put it, "follow your bliss."

In many ways, the "second half" of life is the best time to prepare for your "third half"—the bonus years. Reading this section will help you internalize the perspectives you need to begin this process.

The Quiet Revolution

The time is the 1990s. The place is America. A quiet, yet significant, social revolution is taking place. More and more, people are refusing to retire in the traditional sense.

Life expectancy is lengthening, and for mature adults the *quality* of life is improving even more dramatically. A "third half" of life has appeared.

If you're thinking about getting out, feeling burned out, or being pushed out from your full-time career, you need to be aware of this cultural shift, and you need to plan for it. With the right attitude and preparation, your future years will be the best ones yet.

When you have been caught up in your full-time career—administrator, executive, home-maker, professional, technician—in an office or factory, the public or private sector—looking ahead to your post-career years may be unnerving. Consciously or unconsciously, many people are hesitant to contemplate this period because they don't know what to expect.

Yet, the prospect of more freedom, flexibility, and leisure time has great appeal. People want to change how they spend their time, but more importantly, they want to stay involved and productive. Mature adults nearing the end of the "second half" are realizing that in many ways their full-time careers have been preparing them for their "lifework" in the third half.

AGING AIN'T WHAT IT USED TO BE

A friend of ours recalls: "As a boy, when I visited my grand-mother's house, I remember my *great-grandmother* who was living in a room upstairs. A sweet old lady in her eighties, "still spry" (as they said in those days) and sharp of mind, she always wore black dresses with white lace trim and spent her time tatting (a kind of crochet work). That's the way old people were supposed to dress and act in those days.

"Today, we contrast this memory with a friend who lives out in ski country. He says he was unfit and feeling old when he retired in his sixties, but then he began an exercise regime. Today, in his mid-eighties, he's a well-known skier, both downhill and cross-country, and also a runner. When I expressed surprise one day at his continued activity, he said, 'This is nothing. Last year I competed in the annual race up Pike's Peak!' Someone else exclaimed rather testily, 'Loren, why don't you act your age?' He replied, 'I am.' "

Outmoded stereotypes of older people are collapsing. Even the definition of "aged" is changing; the *old* aren't as old as they used to be! And we are seeing major changes in attitudes toward death and dying.

These changes, in turn, are bringing about a revolution in the concept of retiring. The old goal of "earning" a few final years of rest turned out to be a chimera. Declared Helen Hayes at eighty: "If you rest, you rust." By contrast, the new model is a long, abundant, fulfilling future.

A STATE OF MIND

"You are only as old as you think you are," goes the cliché. But like most clichés, it contains a lot of truth. As the famous baseball great, Satchell Paige, put it, "How old would you be if you didn't know how old you are?" Dr. Ida Davidoff, an octogenarian who at forty had returned to the university to begin work on her Ph.D., told *The New York Times* in an interview, "I feel younger than some ten-year-olds."

An active seventy-year-old woman we know says, "If I don't look in the mirror, I think of myself as not very different from eighteen.

My attitude toward work and play, and even toward men, is the same today as it was then." Another friend, now in her sixties, recalls that as a young mother of twenty-nine, exhausted by her young children, she felt older than she does today. In the same vein, Zorba the Greek, looking back on his youth, said, "I was older then; I am so much younger than that now."

The pages of *Modern Maturity,* the American Association of Retired Persons magazine aimed at the 55-plus audience, are full of people enjoying varied and vital experiences—from riding their Harley-Davidson motorcycles to sailing over the Swiss Alps in a hot-air balloon. So much for the stereotypes of oldsters!

THE OLD MODEL OF RETIREMENT

Until today's quiet revolution, most people, like their parents before them, thought of retirement in traditional terms: the rocking chair, fishing, golf or "just putzing around." In his novel, *The Spectator Bird,* Wallace Stegner gives us an insightful picture of this model of retirement:

JOE ALSTON

Until age sixty, Joe Alston had spent his life as a successful literary agent. Then he retired. It wasn't long before he discovered that the enjoyment and satisfaction of the house and garden "on a wooded lot" that he had dreamed of didn't materialize. He began to feel guilty about his lack of contentment, knowing he should be "as placid as those two deer ruminating my shrubbery up on the hill." Instead, most of the time he was restless, bored, and critical of himself as well as everybody and everything around him. It seemed that he thought mainly about the past, his arthritis, old age and death.

On one of his daily walks, he mused, "My internal grumblings went on the way a high-compression engine running on low-octane gas will go on galloping and coughing after the engine is shut off. It's a bad sign, I know it. Ruth tells me at least once a day that old people, or people getting old, tend to disengage, back away, turn inward, listen only to themselves, and get self-righteous and censorious. And they musn't (that is, I musn't). She hates to drive anywhere with me because I'm inclined to cuss out drivers who don't please me. 'What good does it do?' she cries. 'They can't hear you. All you do is upset me.' 'It lets off steam—failing which I might explode,' I tell her. 'What are you doing now but exploding?' she asks."

Since Joe's retirement, long-suffering Ruth has continued with her own interests: the League of Women Voters, the Town Council and volunteering once a week at a local nursing home. She has tried to get Joe to go there with her. However, the very thought depresses him even more. "I've gone there a couple of times to pick her up and I come out with the horrors. How she stands spending a whole morning among those dim, enfeebled, tottering dead, knowing that she and I are only a few years from being just like them, is beyond my understanding . . . They have asked me to come down and talk to them about books, but I have not gone. I have no more to say to them than if they were refugees from some war, streaming along a road under air attack, diving for the same ditches when they have to, and getting up to struggle on, each for himself."

A GRAND SEDUCTION

Joe Alston is a victim of the very seductive "old model" view that encourages competent, wise and experienced people to think that on an arbitrary given date they should "Go rest, you deserve it." They are led to believe this is what they have worked for all those years. Instead, they interpret this message to mean they are no longer needed or wanted, and many begin to feel they are finished. The thesaurus gives these synonyms for the word "retirement": withdrawal, retreat, regression, departure, abdication, abandonment, solitude, isolation. No wonder Joe is depressed! How different his third half of life might have been if he had done some thinking and planning in advance. And if, in the process, he had realized that satisfaction with life depends on working at something that contributes to society and to the community. Such work is beneficial not only for him but for the world.

As Dr. Robert Butler says of traditional retirement, "Qualities which are especially associated with middle and later life—experience, accumulated skills, knowledge, judgement, wisdom and perspective—are discarded just when they are coming to fruition. Each year as thousands of people are forced to retire, [these qualities] are lost . . ."

MAJOR STRESS

The very act of retiring is traumatic. It is ranked sixth among life's stress-producing experiences, on a par with being jailed or having a major illness. In fact, there is evidence that in some cases, the stress of retirement can actually *cause* major illness.

In the decade leading up to retirement, most people are anxious about what they're going to do with the rest of their lives. Many feel vulnerable and unsure as with any change—but especially today when retirement may mean dealing with twenty to thirty more years.

To make those years count, you need to do four things:

1. Redefine yourself and create a new you, with the understanding that your identity is no longer linked to a job title.
2. Find a way to deal with your "new" environment. Granted, it is your home, but remember, you haven't been around much from Monday to Friday.
3. Find new ways to communicate with those at home while you establish a new turf.
4. Deal with your financial security in a new way.

DEPRESSION AND BOREDOM

Experts on aging Robert N. Butler and Herbert P. Gleason, in their book *Productive Aging—Enhancing Vitality in Later Life,* state, "The unproductive person who is divided from the social role of work is at a higher risk of illness . . . Very often, productivity and health go hand in hand, and they deteriorate together."

Stegner's character, Joe Alston, developed what John Gardner in his book *Self Renewal* terms "mind-forged manacles." Joe is so absorbed in himself and his disappointment at the way his life has turned out, he cannot see beyond it. He has lost his self-confidence; he blames his depression on getting old, when in reality, the source of his sadness is his empty and meaningless life. The focus of his dreams once was on having the perfect place to live—which was sure to make him happy. Now he feels betrayed because the realization of his dream didn't produce the desired effect; inside, he feels restless and discontented. He has lost touch with the Biblical admonition "it is in giving that we receive." Contributing nothing, he is getting nothing. As the saying goes, "A person wrapped up in himself makes a very small package."

OUTDATED PRACTICE

Retirement at age sixty-five is said to have been concocted by Bismarck in Germany over a century ago. In those days, if anyone lived to sixty-five, they were practically in their dotage. The idea was picked up in the United States when Social Security started about sixty years ago. The policy continues to be followed today, despite the fact we can anticipate living at least two decades longer.

In Stegner's novel, Ruth Alston is forced into the role of caregiver by her husband's model. Joe's depression is tiresome and irritating, especially since he persists in ignoring her suggestions about how to feel better. She tries to be patient with him, but ends up feeling helpless and ineffective. Fortunately, she has her own community activities to fall back on. It is no wonder that all kinds of people are joining in today's quiet revolution, making decisions to avoid at all costs the existence that is portrayed in *The Spectator Bird.*

THE NEW MODEL OF RETIREMENT

Thinking about retiring, people used to have just three major concerns: finances, health, location. Now they are concerned with a fourth dimension: how to continue to be productive and useful in some way. This dimension doesn't have to be big and important in the world's view—but it does have to be meaningful to the individual.

DOUG and JANE

Doug was in the legal department of a large corporation, and Jane had a thriving psychotherapy practice, begun when her children left the nest. They decided that when Doug retired, they would sell their suburban home and move to the wonderful old farmhouse in New Hampshire that they had purchased for summer vacations with the family.

In advance of Doug's retirement, they attended a life-planning workshop, where Jane focused on her love of the piano as something she had always wanted to pursue. Doug wanted to continue with his law profession, particularly his interest in ethics and moral values, so he decided to try teaching.

In New Hampshire, where renovating the farmhouse absorbed their initial energies, Jane resumed practicing the piano, becoming good enough to join a local group of musicians. Today, performing with this group, whether for fun or pay, is the joy of her life. Well before their move, Doug had contacted a local college, which hired him to teach law three hours a week, and Civil War history another three hours. He also has become involved in town politics, where his law background is highly appreciated. He has become an avid Civil War buff, reading, learning and taking field trips to the battlefields. He finds he has entered a whole new world of thousands of other people with the same interest. "My only regret," says Doug, "is that this change in my life didn't come sooner, so I could enjoy it longer. I've never been happier."

MARY and ALEX

Mary had a lifelong love of horticulture. When her children left home—long before husband Alex retired—she took courses to earn a certificate in landscape design, and became a professional in the field. After serving in the Air Force right after college, Alex spent thirty years as a financial executive. He claims now that being shut up either in meeting rooms or airplanes gave him a deep yearning "to get out and live in the air, the sky, and the scenery."

The first thing they did after Alex's retirement was buy a

pop-up camper and head west. On that first trip to the mountains they became intrigued with some "pictures on the rocks" —some chiseled, others painted. No one seemed to know much about the images, except that they had been done by early Native Americans. What did they mean? What were the primitive artists trying to say?

Alex and Mary ended up devoting much of their third half of life finding answers to those questions. They have spent much time in New Mexico and Arizona and countless hours in research. They became acquainted with archaeologists and other scientists who were equally fascinated, but were equally baffled by the meaning of the rock art. Subsequently, Alex and Mary made excursions specifically to photograph the rock art, averaging eighty rolls of film and twenty-eight hundred slides each trip, which they sorted, identified, classified, and studied. The result was a book, an anthology of "everything that archaeologists have had to say about rock art in the last 150 years."

Developing a wide acquaintance among local people and scientists, Alex and Mary became recognized as experts. Alex is invited to speak to conventions of archaeologists and others interested in the field. He has embarked on a second book that offers interpretations of the pictures and their meanings. Mary has contributed by photographing the flowers, trees and cactus surrounding the sites—an important aspect of the research that draws on her knowledge of horticulture. Between trips, she maintains her landscape design business.

Alex and Mary say they have happily adopted a new set of values, in which the objective is knowledge, not money. They find it very exciting and satisfying.

STAYING IN THE SWIM

These couples are typical of the new model of retirement. They are doing something that uniquely fits *them,* their interests, talents, and dreams. And they are not unusual. Many people in the third half of life, age fifty-five and beyond, are living useful, productive, satisfying lives. They may be working shorter, more flexible hours that allow more time for leisure, travel, and their families. They are not going out to pasture, they are staying in the swim of things—to mix metaphors!

Never Better

Far from being finished, people in the third half are in their prime. By that time, they know what they are good at—and what they're not—and they know what they enjoy. And, they want to use all this, not put it on the shelf. They have never been better. Life has mellowed them. They have more charity and forgiveness of the shortcomings of others. They have more courage, more strength of their convictions. In short, they are wiser and more mature.

TOO MANY OPTIONS

Your only deterrent may be indecisiveness as to how to spend this precious third half of life. Typically, during the second half you have seized opportunities as they came by, hoping all would turn out well. Approaching the third half may be your first real chance to stand back, look at yourself and consider the options available. This preparation will make a tremendous kind of difference and ideally should be undertaken well ahead of retirement. The couples previously featured did just that. They thought about retirement well beforehand, examined what they loved to do, and used that knowledge to develop a realistic plan.

A "WORK" IN YOUR LIFE

Make sure your plans include productive work. Studs Terkel, author of a book on working, concluded that it is a basic human instinct. This was confirmed by an IBM survey of its annuitants in which eighty-five percent of those who were *not* working wished they were working *some* of the time. This aspect of the quiet revolution is not only good for the mental health and fulfillment of each individual, it is beneficial to society as well. Just imagine what it would mean if the two million people retiring each year (three million by the year 2000) spent part of their time doing something for the public good. Seemingly unsolvable problems might get solved! It is increasingly clear that both the individual and society lose if one's *whole life* is not used productively.

The change agents leading this quiet revolution, people now in their fifties and sixties, are rejecting the traditional approach their parents took to their post-career lives. Called the "silent" generation by some, they are breaking new ground. They are a unique generation with an extraordinary history.

2

A Generation and Its Children

THE SILENT GENERATION

If you were born in the 1920s or 1930s, you are part of what has been dubbed the silent generation. This characterization acknowledges that while your children's generation—the hippies, the baby boomers, the yuppies (terms that didn't even exist when you were young!) —was making a lot of noise and earning widespread attention, you were earnestly working away in the second half of your life. Now that you are about to embark on your third half, you want to make the most of it.

THE "BABY BOOMERS"

If you were born between 1945 and 1965, you are a baby boomer, the huge generation produced promptly after "the boys came marching home" from World War II. Besides the enormous size of your generation, (Ken Dychtwald, author of *Age Wave,* estimates there are seventy-five million of you), you were significant because you were teenagers and young adults in the tumultuous 1960s.

There is a view that three factors formed the basis for that explosive era which changed our lives as Americans—Vietnam, the invention of the "pill," and the assassination of President Kennedy. In any case, as the young often do, you rebelled. You picked up the baton and demanded change. Maybe it was your numbers and the huge noise you made—or more probably, the world was just ready for major change—but where other adolescents demanding change have failed, you succeeded. A social revolution occurred and the world has never been the same since.

Now, another, quieter social revolution is taking place and this time, your parents are at the forefront. Theirs is a unique generation with an extraordinary history. Their life has been very different from that of their industrial age parents, as different as your life has been from theirs. They were the first to break out of the mold in a major way. Perhaps understanding their untold story and its social and economic context will cast some light on how this major change has come to pass and the precedents it sets for you and your future.

TONY

Tony's first memory at age four or five was in 1931 in a small border town in Texas. His father, of Scottish ancestry on both sides for at least five generations, was eking out a living working in a gas station across the street. Before the Great Depression, he had been a sales representative for Standard Oil, a job he had landed after graduating in 1923 from the University of Illinois. After his company let him go, he heard there was work in Texas and moved the family there.

Tony's only memory of Texas was the heat and the starkness of the life there.

His next recollection was of first grade in West Virginia. His father, unable to survive on a gas station attendant's pay, had moved the family again, this time to live with Tony's paternal grandparents. His grandfather, a shoe manufacturer, introduced Tony's father to that business, and in 1935, they moved to Kansas City, where his father became a traveling shoe salesman.

"Times were still hard," Tony recalls. "Doctor and dentist bills were near-catastrophes financially. Mom didn't work, partly because Dad was too proud to let her—wives just didn't work in those days—and partly because jobs were scarce anyway. I see now that we lived in fear and trembling, never knowing if Dad would still have a job the next day. Although he had a salary, it was essentially a 'draw' based on commissions. He spent a lot of time on the road during the week, hanging on by his fingernails."

Tony's father did "make it to some extent" by working sixty-plus hours a week, trying to make enough to "save a little for old age." The choice of Kansas City was a fortuitous one, because the economy depended on agriculture rather than industry. It was a pleasant place to grow up.

"I did well in school. Dad and Mom made sure I did. They pinned their hopes on my success to make up for what Dad considered his failure, I guess. When I was elected senior class president, they were so proud. In those days, annual vacations were short and all we could afford was to visit my grandparents, which I enjoyed anyway. From about fifth grade on, I sold *Saturday Evening Posts* and *Ladies Home Journals* door to door to earn a little spending money; I had no allowance. Summers, I participated in local public parks programs, which were free to residents. I was a Boy Scout and two weeks every summer, I got to go to Scout Camp down in the Ozarks."

A VICTORIAN UPBRINGING IN THE GREAT DEPRESSION

Amid the affluence of the 1990s, it is hard to imagine growing up in an era marked by a general feeling of anxiety and fear that the Great Depression set in motion. Also, children in the silent generation were reared by Victorian-influenced parents who believed that discipline, good behavior, and proper manners were essential to successful development. Tony's mother watched over him closely, not only because she was fearful for her only son, but because she was training him to be a good person. Child psychology was unheard of, and Dr. Spock had not yet published his famous book. Children needed to be "brought up" by parents who "knew best"—and that was that.

No wonder today's grandparents look askance at how far the pendulum has swung as they observe their grandchildren being raised with what seems to be excessive permissiveness and overindulgence. Members of the silent generation generally agree among themselves that growing up in the Depression and the post-Depression era was not all bad. Life was simpler and there were many joys. Children grew up more slowly—a boon that parents of today's TV-influenced kids might envy. (It's been said that if Booth Tarkington wrote his famous novel, *Seventeen,* today, he would have to retitle it *Twelve.*) Families were much more stable, giving children a strong sense of security. *The New York Times* columnist Russell Baker in his two autobiographical books, *Growing Up* and *Good Times,* paints a marvelous, warm, and humorous picture of his childhood in the Depression and his strong, courageous mother who brought him safely through it.

TONY continued

When Tony was in high school, World War II began. Although the Depression was over, its impact remained. "Dad had a company car, which was insured only if he was driving it. That meant I couldn't drive it; Mom didn't need a car because she didn't do much except look after me. I couldn't play football because I might get hurt. Although Kansas City had little crime, my parents kept the doors locked day and night and always locked the car. I got a job as a lifeguard at the municipal swimming pool to earn some money for myself. We ate well and I was nicely clothed, but I definitely felt 'poor.'

"Upon graduating from high school in 1945 at age seventeen, I finally left home for eighteen months in the Army and then went on to college. In the Army, I got interested in international affairs and economics, so instead of going to the state engineering school as I had planned, I applied to a university that had an outstanding economics department. They accepted me and I made it with the help of the GI Bill followed by a scholarship. I also worked my way through school part time, which was good for me. Those were important and enjoyable years that changed my life.

"I had never left home except for brief visits in the summer. My folks still felt insecure themselves and worried a lot about me, too. I wasn't very mature, but I managed to survive, kind of hand-to-mouth. While still in college, I found the right girl and began my second half of life—which turned out to be unbelievably better than the first half!"

WORLD WAR II

Those in the silent generation were the children of the Great Depression and the youths of World War II, which followed almost immediately. Hard times were replaced with fear and dread as German and Japanese forces swept the world. Even those too young for military service were affected. Siblings and friends were killed or missing. The newspapers, magazines and radio were full of war news. There were lots of shortages, and essentials were rationed. The whole nation was mobilized and lived under rules and restrictions.

LIFE-CHANGING BENEFITS

For those who went to war and survived, it often proved to be an enormously enriching and maturing experience. They literally "joined the Navy and saw the world." One man, after going through Naval officer training in Hollywood Beach, Boston and Miami, was assigned to a destroyer escort that was still being built. "Our entire crew was in Norfolk, Virginia, waiting for the ship to be completed," he recalls. "One morning the Captain ordered me to take the men out and drill them. I felt like a scared little kid inside, but I managed to bark out the first order I had ever given in my life! When those sailors snapped to and followed the order, it was the most maturing moment of my life. I grew from a boy to a man—no, to a leader of men—in a single instant. We went on to years of sea duty, to ports on both sides of the Atlantic, to the Mediterranean and Italy and North Africa . . . I wouldn't trade my years in the Navy for anything in the world."

Like Tony, many returning service men were able to have a college education they might otherwise have missed, courtesy of the GI Bill.

THE COLD WAR

On the heels of World War II, the forty-year Cold War between the United States and Russia began. International crises and the overshadowing fear of destruction continued to be the order of the day for the silent generation. When Tony and his wife Ann were first married, some of their friends were building bomb shelters. "I remember one evening sitting on our patio with a knot in the pit of my stomach as I pictured in my mind the total destruction of New York if the Russians decided to lob over an ICBM," Tony recalled. A few years later, they faced the Cuban missile crisis: "When President Kennedy dispatched warships to turn back the Soviet missile ship, the whole country held its breath. I wondered, does this mean war again?"

THE STRAIGHT AND NARROW

The young men in this generation typically went straight into jobs after military service or college. Tony married his college sweetheart, Ann, six months after graduation—having earned just enough for a honeymoon with a few dollars left over. Salaries were modest, there was no money for frills and most couples lived frugally, influenced in many cases by advice from parents who feared another economic depression. The work ethic prevailed. A husband and father's first responsibility was to his family. In actuality, that usually meant his career came first. Many men stayed with the same company for thirty years, working hard to get to the top.

This lock-step progression from Depression-era childhood and adolescence to wartime youth to college to marriage and into a career—without a pause—meant these men never had the freedom of today's young people. There was little opportunity for sewing wild oats. And when the men of this silent generation began to turn forty, there was a heavy reckoning as this unlived part of their lives surfaced. Their regrets and the feeling that they had missed something were summed up poignantly in a sign carried by a member of the class of '45 at a college reunion: "Born thirty-five years too soon."

A GENERATION AND ITS CHILDREN

TONY and ANN

The story of Tony's sweetheart, Ann, is quite typical of women of the silent generation. After a happy childhood in a family who loved her, she went to a woman's college. It was during this time that she met Tony. After dating for two years while in college, they made plans to be married as soon as possible after graduation. "This was what was expected of girls at the time," Ann says, "and it was a relief because I had no idea what I would do after college otherwise. They didn't even offer typing at my college." After their marriage, Tony and Ann moved to a strange city, where they soon began a family.

Looking back, Ann says, "I was on my own all day long for the first time in my life. There was no one from my world nearby, and I had nothing to do. The biggest event in my week was going for the weekly groceries. I had no skills, no interests besides Tony, and really no idea about myself or what I wanted out of life, except children. That problem solved itself, because my first baby came soon and was the prime objective in my life." Two more children followed, and from then on, her personal interests were on hold for twenty years.

Ann's midlife crisis came when she began to realize her children were growing up fast and would soon fly the nest. "What could I possibly do 'out there'? I began to see I had never really become an individual before I married. I'd always been dependent on someone, having gone, in effect, from my father to my husband. I had been a daughter, sister, wife and mother—and was proud of how I had performed in all these roles. But who was I, really, without all these people? What might I do that I would enjoy and would be useful to people? I had no idea. It was scary."

SILENT GENERATION WOMEN

Many more women in the silent generation attended college than ever before. Socially, however, college was more or less a continuation of high school. There were still rules: girls had little opportunity to develop self-responsibility; the freedom that is taken for granted by girls today was unthinkable. Colleges didn't offer subjects to prepare women for future careers, and only rarely did a woman study to enter a profession other than teaching or nursing.

After marriage, the women stayed home to raise their families. Their first priorities were husband, children, and home. Women's magazines of the day portrayed the ideal wife as a perfect mother who not only had beautiful children, but was a Girl Scout leader and taught Sunday school. She was an excellent cook, could decorate a home beautifully, arrange flowers, entertain well, and create a gorgeous garden.

Underneath all this, many women experienced feelings of restlessness, frustration, and even guilt that they were not enjoying it more! As one woman put it, "I was overeducated and undertrained to be a housewife." There was a yearning to do something more with their minds. At the age of forty-five, when their children went off to college or beyond, but their husbands were still deep in their careers, these women began to reach for personal freedom and search for fulfillment. They plunged into educational programs, some even into professional degrees—laying the groundwork, as it turns out, for the third half of their lives.

Ann was one of these women. At forty-nine, she returned to school, which she enjoyed, and five years later, received her graduate degree in teaching. Now she has settled on a job in the local school system, where she looks forward not only to the students but to new friendships in the faculty. She feels her life is fuller now, and she is excited about the future.

THE NEW WORLD—DRUGS, SEX, AND REBELLION

After all the traumas the silent generation had lived through, they ran smack into the social turbulence of "the sixties" as their own children reached adolescence. Through their sons and daughters, these parents were exposed to "the pill" and the sexual revolution; the Vietnam War, peace demonstrations, and campus uprisings; and drugs, a totally unfamiliar, incomprehensible force that attacked, and sometimes ruined, their offspring. For a long time, schools either ignored the drug problem or pushed it off on parents, who had no idea where to turn. They felt ashamed and disgraced, and above all, they felt helpless.

The Vietnam debacle led to a general disillusionment among young people toward government, churches, corporations, and universities—the institutions their parents had respected and defended blindly. Communication between the generations broke down.

A NEW WORLD FOR PARENTS

Nardi Reeder Campion summed it up thus in a 1989 piece in *The New York Times:* "My generation deserves a medal for surviving the sex revolution. Since I graduated from college in 1938, for us, the word 'sex' meant 'male' or 'female' on a driver's license . . . My generation has gone from the morals of Herbert Hoover to the morals of Gary Hart; from 'Rebecca of Sunnybrook Farm' to 'The Mayflower Madam;' from storks and cabbage patches to surrogate mothers and test-tube fathers; from Emily Post to Dr. Ruth; from the once-unmentionable topic, homosexuality, to Gay Rights; from 'It Happened One Night' to 'Sammy and Rosie Get Laid.' "

From the distance of a quarter of a century, some people are able to joke now about the sixties. But for parents of adolescents in that era, it was a nightmare, a time of real suffering.

THE FIRST SANDWICH GENERATION

At the same time that the silent generation was trying to deal with their children's changing values, they had to cope with their aging parents' declining years. Having lived before our present-day knowledge of, and emphasis on, health and fitness, and having scrimped and saved for a few years of total leisure—which turned out to be decades of self-indulgent emptiness—these aging parents sometimes ended up physically ill or mentally disillusioned and sad. Too often, they were emotionally and even financially dependent on their now-adult children—a situation that wasn't much fun for either party. When one of the parents inevitably died, the surviving spouse, lacking interests other than him- or herself, faced an even emptier and more lonely future.

NEW CUSTOMS AND VALUES

Finally, as the children of the silent generation matured, they had new customs and values that were hard for their Victorian-reared parents to swallow. They had live-in partners, officially dubbed POSSLQs (persons of the opposite sex sharing living quarters). They frequently seemed to have more money than their parents ever dreamed of having at the same age, which they spent lavishly, to their Depression-bred parents' dismay. Or, while temporarily finding themselves, these young adults moved back home with their parents —always a stressful situation.

TONY'S MIDLIFE CRISIS

By age fifty-five, Tony has been with a blue chip corporation for twenty-five years. Having risen to middle management, he considers himself a success in his business career. He enjoys his work as well as his colleagues with whom he has lunched and bantered all these years. He has attained the financial security that was his goal.

But below the surface, all is not ideal. Although Tony feels he is good at his job and has more knowledge and experience than most of those around him, he hasn't had a promotion in eight years. In fact, he has been passed over for several positions he had his eye on and felt he was in line for. His career seems to have gone dead, and he feels slightly bored with his job. The last time he talked to his boss, he was assured everything was fine. However, he feels restless and has begun to think about leaving.

Then a good friend who had just retired died suddenly of a heart attack. Shocked, Tony has found himself thinking, for the first time ever, about his own death. He has even dreamt about it.

When Tony thinks about retiring, he doesn't know what he would do. He's heard it is impossible for people over forty-five to find another corporate job. Maybe he should just hang it up, he thinks, and move to Phoenix or somewhere and just play golf. "I deserve it," he says, "after all these years of slogging away." When Tony has mentioned this idea to Ann, he has gotten little response. She gets quiet and changes the subject.

Fact is, Ann is close to panic. Realizing that her husband is increasingly bored and frustrated, she is concerned. He has become quieter and more thoughtful. When she has gotten him to talk about it, he has told her of being passed over. Maybe he should retire, he suggests. Ann sees the new life she is planning going out the window. She doesn't want to move. After all she has done to start her new career here at home, the thought of starting over leaves her weak.

She finds herself impatient with Tony, wishing he would cheer up. She almost dreads his coming in the door at night, and begins to wonder what it would be like to have him around all the time. This makes her feel guilty because they've always had a good marriage and Tony has been her life. Yet looking back, between his working and her preoccupation with the children growing up, they have lived somewhat separate lives. They haven't discussed things much. She catches herself wondering, "What would we talk about if we were together all the time?"

The next time Tony mentions "retiring to Phoenix or somewhere," Ann tries to discourage him from leaving. She suggests that a two-week or month-long vacation would be grand, but longer wouldn't be a good idea at this time. Tony, although he loves golf and finds the thought of more leisure in his life appealing, cannot picture getting up in the morning and not going to work. He knows Ann is right: his work is his life and he can't leave it right now. He decides to tough it out awhile longer, though the zest is gone. Much relieved, Ann begins her career.

EXIT MENTALITY VERSUS RE-ENTRY

Tony and Ann's story, like Joe and Ruth Alston's from chapter 1, illustrates the opposite goals of many men and women at this juncture in life. Men have an "exit mentality," thinking of leaving their careers and slowing down. Women, free of home and family responsibilities at last, are eager to *start* a career. Women are more practiced than men at adjusting to major changes. They have lived through babies becoming children and going off to school, and then becoming adults and leaving home. Each time, with each child, the mother has had to adjust.

Now, at this juncture, both men and women experience the shock of awareness of growing older. Loss of agility and endurance, or a sudden serious illness, forces them to take stock. They can no longer hide *from themselves* the fact that the advancing years are catching up with them.

Tony and Ann are experiencing what Gail Sheehy termed "midlife crisis." They had worked long and hard to get where they were, but now they're questioning their own values, where they're going and why. Is this the happiness they'd been looking for? Is this all there is? The prayer of the person in the midlife crisis is, "Lord, don't let me die before I've really lived."

Now in their fifties and sixties, the silent generation has survived a succession of crises and adjusted to one tumultuous change after another. Throughout time, according to historian Arnold Toynbee, crises have been caused by disequilibrium and major world change; and these crises, in turn, have brought about growth. If this is true, then the silent generation should be outstanding!

FREEDOM

Standing at last on the threshold of the third half of life, they feel great. They see that the next twenty-five to thirty years ahead could be the best years of all. They have good health, freedom, and (because they have worked hard and saved) more money in their pockets than any generation before. The kids are educated and the mortgage is paid. From their own aging parents, they have seen the pitfalls of a life of leisure and they reject the traditional model of retirement. Still, the question looms: What now?

As we said at the beginning of this chapter, there are no precedents for the silent generation. They are pioneers, breaking new ground. They are creating a new paradigm. They are purposeful, action-oriented, eager to make the most of this new freedom. What they are about to experience is not "growing old," but rather "older growing."

3

Older Growing

*At the root of human responsibility is the concept of perfection,
the urge to achieve it, the intelligence to find a path toward it,
and the will to follow that path.*
                                        —*Aung San Suu Kyi*

When you're through changing, you're through.
                                        —*Bruce Barton*

To believe that a curtain drops on life at age sixty or sixty-five,
leaving nothing to do but play golf or shuffleboard, makes no sense
at all. Not only does that attitude and behavior fail to bring personal
satisfaction in the long run, it is inconsistent with recognized theories
of evolution and human development, which conclude that the purpose of life is to grow and mature until the day you die.

HUMAN DEVELOPMENT

Prior to the work of Charles Darwin in the late nineteenth century,
little attention was paid to how human beings develop. But Darwin's
theories touched off a torrent of interest and research by scientists,
historians, and theologians, leading eventually to the "human potential movement" of the present day.

During the first half of the twentieth century, three European
geniuses in three different disciplines pioneered this field. Although

each worked independently, their theories, taken together, constitute a philosophy of life. They demonstrate a pattern and meaning to life. Equally important, they show that growth and development—of both society and individuals—does not stop at some arbitrary point, but continues in spite of adversities.

ARNOLD TOYNBEE'S PATTERNS IN HISTORY

English historian Arnold Toynbee studied the history of civilization from a large perspective. He divided world history into twenty-six civilizations and traced how each had risen, flourished, begun to decline, and finally, fallen. He theorized that internal disequilibrium and breakdowns caused crises that brought about growth. Through death and rebirth processes, the world has slowly improved and progressed.

TEILHARD DE CHARDIN'S EVOLUTION IN NATURE

French priest and biologist Teilhard de Chardin studied the relationship of nature to man. He wrote prolifically, until his death at age eighty-five, about the concepts that emerged from his research. He reached four inspiring conclusions relevant to older growing.

- He perceived a dynamic expansion of consciousness within the universe. Even rocks, as well as trees and other plants, constantly evolve toward higher forms of being. Through this process, which he called "cosmogenesis," the whole cosmos is going toward more light and life.
- He observed that the more evolved something is, the more complex it is. Rocks are the simplest, trees and plants are much more complex, animals still more, and man is the most evolved and the most complex.
- He had sublime faith that matter and energy are always in progression, that there is an unbroken pattern of growth and development of the planet from the beginning of time until now.
- Teilhard concluded that the purpose of life is growth, an evolving higher consciousness.

CARL JUNG ON UNDERSTANDING HEALTHY HUMAN DEVELOPMENT

Swiss psychiatrist Carl Jung concentrated his research on people—and his stature and influence have increased enormously with the passage of time. Having worked with Freud, Jung concluded that Freud's focus on childhood's effect on adult problems and his focus on mental illness were too narrow. While Jung, too, dealt with psychopathology, he was profoundly interested in understanding healthy human development and the inner and outer forces—social institutions, mythology, and religion—which influence it.

Among his many significant conclusions, three are pertinent here:

- Early in life, a person is mostly unconscious—and the unconscious mind is where one's innate potential resides. It is important, therefore, for the person to become constantly more conscious. The more aware one becomes, the more one grows toward maturity, the more an individual's hidden power is released. Jung believed that each step of growth makes a person more conscious and throws more light into the unconscious mind.
- The first step of growth, and hence the first opportunity for psychological change for most individuals, is the difficult transition from childhood and adolescence to adulthood. The personality then grows slowly from age twenty to about forty, when the next major change occurs. The difficult challenge here is to adapt from young adulthood to the reality of approaching old age. This "midlife change," according to Jung, is when the search begins for the purpose of life and when the person acquires wholeness and maturity. Over a period of years, one seeks to become more uniquely the individual one is meant to be.
- Jung perceived that each step of growth leads people to become more like themselves and less like anyone else. At the same time, although each person is unique, we all live in the community, and need to relate to and work with other people in order to grow. He saw the reconciliation of these opposites as the primary task of our lives.

Following the European work, several American psychologists picked up where their predecessors left off and succeeded in popularizing the subject of personal development.

ERIK ERIKSON'S HUMAN LIFE CYCLE

Erik Erikson, a student of Jung's, carried on the master's work, originating a concept he called the "life cycle." He saw each person's life cycle as consisting of eight stages of psychological development, with each stage having a specific task that had to be completed (before moving on to the next stage), in order to progress to full maturity. Erikson's life cycle stages and their accompanying tasks are:

Stage	Task
Childhood stages:	
Infancy	Find basic trust
Early childhood	Separate from mother
Play age	Learn to take initiative
School age	Become educated
Adolescence	Gain a sense of identity
Adult stages:	
Young adulthood	Learn how to achieve intimacy
Adulthood	Care-giving
Old age	Establishing integrity

Erickson clarified this last task as learning to "say it as you see it," not caring what others think. Originally, he defined the "old age" stage as being over sixty-five. However, when he himself was well into that stage and discovered how young he really was at sixty-five, he added another stage, eighty and beyond. He drew the inspiring conclusion that those in this stage reap the rewards of completing all the previous tasks—wisdom, maturity, serenity, and peace of mind for as long as the future holds.

DANIEL LEVINSON ON CRISIS AND ITS VALUE IN A MAN'S LIFE

In his book, *The Seasons of a Man's Life,* psychologist Daniel Levinson refined Erikson's work, continuing intensive research into the life cycle theory. He concluded that we do not develop in a continuous, unchanging flow, but that life is made up of relatively long "seasons," which he compared to acts of a play. He observed that in order for each of these "acts" to close and the next one to begin, there must be a crisis or turning point—a serious illness, the death of a loved one, divorce, loss of a job or, yes, retirement! The Greek root of the word "crisis" means "change," and such changes are necessary for new learning and new growth to take place. Turning points are opportunities for attaining higher states of consciousness and progress toward wholeness and maturity.

GAIL SHEEHY ON AGES AND STAGES OF LIFE

Gail Sheehy, a protégé of Margaret Mead and author of the best-selling book *Passages,* contributed her own view of the developmental stages of women as well as men. Sheehy's book had three major objectives:

- To pinpoint people's *inner* changes in response to changes in the outside world.
- To reveal the differences in how men and women develop, showing how unsynchronized their stages are and how different their tempo.
- To predict and examine the resulting crises within couples' relationships.

For example, in the silent generation at least, as men in their twenties typically were working out in the world and gaining confidence, their wives were tied down at home with the children, losing their self-assurance about worldly matters. Later, when the husband was ready to settle down, his wife was beginning to get restless. And when the man in his forties was entering his midlife crisis, feeling his dreams, power, and illusions slipping away, the woman was eager to get out and conquer the world.

THE HUMAN BRAIN

Basic to the whole concept of older growing is the new knowledge about how our brains work. Actually, Swiss psychologist Jean Piaget made the first breakthrough early in the twentieth century. In studies on how children learn, he proved that contrary to widespread belief, memory does not deteriorate over time. Instead, it can even improve by acquiring certain intellectual skills. Subsequent research by chemists, molecular biologists and physicists has provided immense insight into how the brain functions.

Interestingly, Peter Russell in his *The Brain Book* reports that extensive research supports the view of Piaget and others that human growth and development need never stop—indeed, it *ought* never stop. Russell states, "The human brain is the most complex and most powerful information processor known to man. Unlike an electronic computer, the brain can carry on a thousand different functions simultaneously, continually cross-referencing and integrating new information. Though many times more powerful and flexible than a computer, the brain weighs only three and a half pounds."

The human brain is not analogous to a telephone exchange, where you simply plug into certain centers for messages; nor is it like a computer, which responds in certain established ways to given stimuli. For learning, the brain employs an electrochemical process in which ten billion neurons are interacting and connecting, with current experiences and stimuli hooking into older memories.

Learning, in Russell's words, involves "coherent patterns of electrical activity in millions of pathways moving over the brain as a whole . . . electrical changes which result in changes in protein synthesis in the neurons." It is probably the most complex system in the universe, which makes its potential for learning almost unlimited. Most of us probably use only a fraction of our mental potential.

Learning and memory are different mental processes, memory being the most important because it is involved in everything we do. Russell states, "Memory is not like a container that gradually fills up. It is more like a tree which is constantly growing hooks onto which the memories are hung. Everything you remember is another set of hooks on which still more new memories can be attached—so the capacity of memory *keeps on growing. The more you know, the more you can know."*

MIND-SET

One important revelation of the new research into the brain has to do with "mind-set." Science has proven conclusively, according to

Russell, that you tend to see what you expect to see, and to miss seeing what you are not expecting. Because of mind-set, many beliefs about the world or other people are self-validating. You notice whatever supports your belief, automatically fulfilling the goals you set for yourself. If bad things always seem to be happening to you, it may well be because of a pessimistic self-image. Conversely, deliberately "setting" yourself for positive goals can bring success. Thus, ironically, science has proved Norman Vincent Peale's writing on "the power of positive thinking." This principle is illustrated in a homely, little parable:

> In a town that shall remain nameless, a visitor pulls his car into a service station and asks the operator, "Can you tell us what this town is like? Is it a good place to live? We're considering moving here." The service station man counters with, "What's the matter with the town where you live now?"
>
> "Oh," says the visitor, "it's a lousy town. The people are narrow-minded and arrogant and disagreeable. In fact, our neighbors are so bad we're in a lawsuit with 'em. That's one reason we want to move."
>
> "Well," replies the operator, "to tell you the truth, I'm afraid you wouldn't find this town any better. You'd meet people pretty much like you describe. I don't think you'd be happy here."
>
> Later that same day, another visitor drives up and asks, "Mister, can you tell us what this town is like? Is it a good place to live? We are being transferred." The service station man asks, "What is the town like that you're moving from?"
>
> "Oh," cries the visitor, "it's just a grand place to live. The people are so warm and friendly and helpful We have the greatest neighbors! We hate to have to leave!"
>
> "Well," replies the operator, "you're in luck. This is just that same kind of town. You'll meet the nicest people. I know you'll be happy living here."

Ralph Waldo Emerson knew about "set" way back in the nineteenth century. He wrote, "No man can learn what he has not preparation for learning . . . A chemist may tell his most precious secrets to a carpenter and he shall be never the wiser—secrets he would not utter to a chemist for an estate. God screens us from premature ideas. Our eyes . . . cannot see things that stare us in the face until the hour arrives when the mind is ripened—then we behold them, and the time we saw them not is like a dream."

RIGHT BRAIN/LEFT BRAIN DOMINANCE

Another discovery about the brain has relevance here. The brain has two distinctive hemispheres: the left side operates in the linear, step-by-step manner used for language or mathematics; the right side has an intuitive, nonrational character that is used in the arts. One side of the brain is dominant in every individual. This discovery is significant in our awareness of our own talents and shortcomings. Schools traditionally emphasize the left hemisphere, teaching the three Rs through step-by-step thinking and logic. This is fine for a left-brain child, but agony for a right-brain kid! Children who have a creative, holistic view of life, or children who are near-prodigies in music or art, are made to feel dumb in left-brain-oriented schools. As right-brain students fall behind in traditional subjects, they may acquire a sense of failure that will increase as they grow older.

Right-brain-dominant kids need their intuitive thinking reinforced in the beginning of their schooling, according to Elaine de Beauport, founder of the Mead School for Human Development in Greenwich, Connecticut. Their abilities need to be affirmed for them to feel successful. In other words, if they can be given a positive set early on, it can be applied to more difficult subjects later.

KEEP ON LEARNING

Neurologically, there is no reason for mental abilities, once gained, ever to decline. The only apparent reasons for decline are disease, disuse, or decline of *expectations to learn.* In fact, our mental abilities should improve throughout life. Still, Joe Alston from chapter 1 is probably typical of the way many older people feel. He believes that society finds him an expense and an embarrassment, and wishes he would disappear into some retirement home or "retreat to a shuffleboard court in some balmy climate." All the while, his problem is simply that he isn't using his intellect any more.

Consider a study by the National Institute on Aging on the mental skills of four thousand people, as reported in *The New York Times* in 1986:

- While many older people do have some loss of mental skills, it is *because of disuse* rather than physical impairment.
- When some fuzziness in problem-solving or numerical and verbal skills occurred, it could be reversed by tutoring tailored to the individual's strengths and weaknesses.
- Some older people reported that young people treated them as doddering and incompetent. But the solution was obviously to change the set of the minds of both the oldsters and the young people observing them.

For example:

> *Alice Phillip noticed in her sixties and seventies that she wans't remembering things. She wondered if her brain was getting rusty and that "this was just the way my mind worked." She began taking suggested mental exercises to improve reasoning skills. Not only did she improve them, but regained skills she had thought lost and discovered some she didn't even know she had! As a result, she began feeling much better about herself and projected her new image to younger people around her. At seventy-eight, she wrote a book entitled,* A Guide to Independent Living.

The greatest obstacles to older growing are these persistent, insidious, and destructive myths:

- Myth #1—Intelligence and memory decrease as we age.
- Myth #2—We no longer change and develop after adulthood.
- Myth #3—After age forty-five, we are pretty much in a decline and should settle for a life of leisure.

To combat these myths, we must first avoid slipping into that thinking ourselves. We should seek to constantly learn new things and, if necessary, practice proven methods of retrieving the material stored in our memory. We need to adopt and nurture new attitudes. We need to create a new, positive mind-set. What we expect in our older years is what we will get. The future is as bright and exciting as we want to make it.

BEATING THE AGE GAME

Actually, this perspective is nothing new—Henry Wadsworth Longfellow had it when he wrote this poem for the fiftieth anniversary of the Class of 1825 at Bowdoin College:

> But why, you ask me, should this tale be told
> To men grown old, or who are growing old?
> It is too late! Ah, nothing is too late
> Till the tired heart shall cease to palpitate.
> Cato learned Greek at eighty; Sophocles
> Wrote his grand *Oedipus,* and Simonides
> Bore off the prize of verse from his compeers
> When each had numbers more than fourscore Years.
> And Theophrastes, at fourscore and ten
> Had but begun his *Characters of Men.*
> Chaucer, at Woodstock with the nightingales,
> At sixty wrote the *Canterbury Tales*;
> Goethe at Weimar, toiling to the last,
> Completed Faust when eighty years were past.
> These are indeed exceptions, but they show
> How far the gulf-stream of our youth may flow
> Into the artic regions of our lives,
> Where little else than life itself survives.

When you reach the third half of your life, look for this kind of creativity in yourself. You have it within you to continue to evolve and produce. Take on new challenges, both mental and physical. Stretch yourself. Too much leisure and too much relaxation are dangerous to your health! Replace growing older with older growing! And, as chapter 4 shows, we believe the data proves that one necessity in this new way of life is to continue some kind of work.

4

Redefining "Work"

In the last analysis, the essential thing is the life of the individual. This alone makes history. Here alone do the great transformations first take place, and the whole future—the whole history of the world—ultimately springs as a gigantic summation from these hidden sources in individuals. In our most private and subjective lives, we are not only the passing witness of our age . . . but also its makers.

— *Carl Jung*

The purpose of life is to serve and to show compassion and the will to help others. Only then have we ourselves become true human beings.

— *Albert Schweitzer*

Yes, culture and civilizations have been built by the work lives of individuals. And work is the essential element in your relationship to your world and the fulfillment of your life—in the third (as well as the second) half of your life.

THE SEDUCTIONS OF RETIREMENT

David Brown, who is well into the third half of his life, is still working. He is the highly successful producer of such hit movies as *Jaws, The Sting, Cocoon* and, most recently, *The Player.* He is married to the editor-in-chief of *Cosmopolitan,* Helen Gurley Brown. In his sassy, irreverent book *Brown's Guide to Growing Gray,* he quotes the fabled literary agent Irving "Swifty" Lazar, over eighty years old, who woke up one morning thinking, "If I didn't have something to do today, I'd rather be dead."

Brown continues, "If you don't have something to do today, you *are* dead. You are not only dead but are also in a purgatory of boredom. Nobody needs you. No matter how your bones creak or what difficulty you have getting out of bed, I recommend that you *work yourself to death. It's the only way to live.*

"Years ago, I had the good luck to have made enough money never to have to work again. I was tempted by the idea. I tried spending seven days without responsibility, duties or deadlines at an island resort in the Caribbean. Within hours I was consulting airline schedules back to snowy, slushy Manhattan. Today, when somebody, seeing me at five in the morning on a remote film location, asks why I still work, my standard reply is, 'If I didn't, who would have lunch with me?' "

Think about that reply for a moment. There's a lot of wisdom in it.

Declares Brown flatly, "Almost everybody I know who feels young, vital and sexy—no matter what their age—is working. Armand Hammer, in his late eighties, was making plans for his nineties. Robert Penn Warren became our first poet laureate at eighty. Dancer Martha Graham was still choreographing at ninety-four. George Burns is booked to play London's Palladium when he's a hundred. 'How can I die when I'm booked?' he quips."

Retirement is a siren song promising an idyllic life of leisure without pressures or responsibilities, but in reality, one often ends up a wreck on the shoals of boredom, feeling useless. Work, on the other hand, often connotes doing something you *have* to do to earn money rather than something you *want* to do for satisfaction, self-worth, and simply to make the world a better place. Work has gotten a bum rap.

A WORN-OUT TAPE

This is perhaps not surprising from an historical viewpoint. For thousands of years, survival for the vast majority required dawn-todusk labor in the fields and vineyards, first at the tribal level and later as serfs under the domination of a feudal lord. After the industrial revolution, the misery shifted to factories, mines, and sweatshops that wore people out early. Later, even in shops and offices, the hours were long and the work was dull and tedious. Indeed, it was against this background that age sixty-five was established as the time work life should end and Social Security payments should begin.

WHY WORK?

In the last half of the twentieth century, three-quarters of the American population is classified as middle income, meaning they are educated and have some choice as to what work they will pursue and where. People in our time work for two main reasons: first, to make enough income to live, preferably in the lifestyle they want, and second, to express who they are, to have an intrinsic feeling of self-worth, and to do something that helps others, or contributes to the good of the world.

"Aw, come on," you say, "most people aren't that public-spirited, philanthropic, and idealistic." Maybe they aren't, consciously. But the economists will tell you that *every* job on earth contributes to the value of the whole. Human beings working together transform physical materials into goods or perform services which benefit other human beings. That's the only reason the recipients of those goods or services are willing to pay for them, which, in turn, pays the worker's wage or salary. Whatever a worker earns in return for his efforts or talents is a direct reflection of his contribution to society outside and beyond his family. (On the other hand, actual monetary reward for work does not necessarily reflect one's individual assessment of its value and contribution to humankind.

Whether a person's motive for working is to serve or to maintain a standard of living—or some of both—the advent of the information age has turned the tables. Office and factory tedium is being replaced with mental stimulation and challenge. Work has even become too absorbing for some people, leading to the promotion and expansion of Workaholics Anonymous!

NEW HORIZONS

If you are in the third half of your life or about to enter it, you have more work choices than ever before. Instead of having to work for financial security, you have to make a conscious decision to work in a world where leisure has become a major, if misplaced goal. At this period in your life you may wish to continue in the field you know best—if you enjoy it—or enter an entirely different field that can be fulfilling and fun. You can work and achieve a new balance of work and leisure in your life. It can be for pay, to supplement your other retirement income. Or you may choose an unpaid job that offers you great satisfaction and a sense of accomplishment.

BILL and CAROL

Bill and Carol grew up and were married in the midwest. Bill knew he enjoyed teaching, so after serving in World War II, he returned to his university for a master's degree in education. However, when a good opportunity with a large company turned up, he took it. After a thirty-five-year career in business, Bill retired. By that time, he and Carol had four children and had lived in six countries around the world.

Typical of women of her generation, Carol's life had focused on managing their home and raising the family. During the last decade of Bill's career, back in the United States and with her children in school, Carol was able to return for education and training in her lifelong interest: interior design.

When Bill was fifty-five, he was given an incentive to retire, so he took it. He and Carol had never made plans for retirement, so having no roots anywhere, they picked a city with a good climate and a location they liked, and moved there. With a secure financial situation and a golf course at the back door of their new home, they looked forward to playing lots of golf, which they both enjoyed, and to meeting people on the links. Life in retirement seemed idyllic.

Soon after moving in, Carol met a woman looking for a partner in her decorating business. Carol jumped at the chance, and within six months was deeply into a new career, feeling in many ways happier and freer than ever in her life.

Bill, on the other hand, after a few months began to feel restless, bored, and a little depressed. He began to talk about moving again, starting a bed-and-breakfast inn somewhere in the country or investing in real estate that he could develop. Carol was sympathetic, but having relocated so often and now loving her new job, she had no desire to move again—and frankly was horrified at the idea of toiling in a bed-and-breakfast inn in the hinterland. Tension began to build between them to the point that Bill threatened to go and do it anyway.

At this time, the couple attended our life planning seminar where they were able to individually and objectively stand back and think out their lives and future. Bill, in particular, realized his life was empty and that he was bored with it and himself. He faced up to the fact that he needed work in his life to give it purpose. He remembered his early love of teaching and determined to pursue it.

That was several years ago. Today, Bill is running a second-language educational program for disadvantaged people, and providing them with personal tutoring. Carol's decorating business is prospering. They still make time to play golf and are completely settled and satisfied. And Bill hasn't mentioned his bed-and-breakfast idea again.

DAVID

David had everything going for him. Coming from an advantaged background, he received an excellent education in prestigious schools, served as an officer in World War II, married well, and landed a good job with a public relations firm. He went swiftly up the ladder to become president of the company at age forty-one. He found his job challenging and satisfying.

Suddenly, at age sixty, his wife divorced him and his company was taken over. He soon found himself out on the street. The shock was enormous. He had made the common mistake of identifying himself with his job title, and now that identity was lost. He had never been on the other side of the desk, never had to look for a job. He turned to friends and contacts in his industry, but they told him they had nothing for him. He perceived it was because he was too old.

He began to realize that almost half of his adult life was still ahead of him. What was he to do with it? For the first time in his life, he began to feel depression, uncertainty, and fear. He lost his confidence and his depression deepened. Fortunately, David sought therapy and after a period of treatment, he was able to find himself again. He learned to put the past behind him and address the future.

He became involved as a volunteer with three separate organizations working in the inner city that needed his particular skills and energy. Although he had always thought in terms of paid jobs, he didn't really *need* the income, and he began to feel great inner satisfaction from the appreciation he received from the paid staffs. His confidence has returned, his depression has disappeared, and today, he says these jobs are the most important and satisfying things he has ever done.

If, in your third half, you choose to remain in the business world, you may be more welcome than you think. A survey of medium-size U.S. companies produced these sample responses:

> . . . *We find 'over fifties' have sounder priorities than younger people.*
> . . . *Can't teach experience; there's no substitute for mature thought.*
> . . . *Older hires are more loyal, better able to deal with complexity.*

You may also find you are in good company. Mike Wallace of *60 Minutes* and Don Hewitt, program producer, both recently signed contracts that will take them into their seventies. More than eighty chief executive officers of Fortune 500 companies are over sixty-five.

The desirability of working in the third half of life is a common concept among politicians. Margaret Thatcher said on her retirement, "Life begins at sixty-five. I shall be working for the future." Ronald Reagan served his two terms as U.S. president after he turned seventy. Shirley Povich, sports columnist for *The Washington*

Post, focused on his favorite pastimes of fishing, travel, and golf after leaving the newspaper, but he says, "The truth is, I missed working." So he went back to writing two or three columns a month instead of his former six per week. He muses, "I found my own way to deal with retirement. I retired it."

There is no age limit to creative expression. Michelangelo was in his late eighties when he painted the ceiling of the Sistine Chapel. In their nineties, Albert Schweitzer and Pablo Casals were still very active. Victor Borge is in his eighties. At seventy-nine, Ignacy Paderewski was still playing the piano magnificently to large audiences. Until he died at ninety-three, Bernard Baruch was still advising presidents. Isaac Asimov, the most prolific author of our time, once wrote, "It has always been my ambition to die with my head face down on a keyboard with my nose caught between two of the keys." He almost made it: his 466th book was published only a month before he died at seventy-two.

IT'S GOOD FOR YOUR HEALTH

Some of you may be saying, "Hey, aren't you painting a rosy picture? I've lost some hearing and my memory isn't what it used to be. What about illness?"

Certainly there are some afflictions of advancing age. You may fall victim to a disease. (So do young people.) But statistics show that three out of four people *over seventy-five* are in good health and are more likely to remain that way if they *do something with their lives.*

Advances in health care have led not only to longer lives, but to more healthy lives. Not long ago, if a man retired at sixty-five, he could expect only ten more years—and was tired both physically and mentally. In the 1990s, a man is more likely to "retire" at fifty-five to sixty, and in peak condition—so he can expect to be around for another twenty-five to thirty years. Health and wellness are dealt with at length in chapter 13.

PROCTOR

Proctor came from a prominent family in Wichita, Kansas. Upon graduation from the state university, where he had been a leader, he joined the family construction business. He married, and he and his wife had several children.

Then in 1952, Proctor was stricken with polio in the epidemic that occurred just before the discovery of the Salk vaccine. He was completely paralyzed from the neck down. He remained strapped to a board during the day, absolutely dependent on constant care by nurses and aides. But Proctor refused to give up and devised a specially equipped large van with a crane to hoist him in and out so he could have mobility. Able to turn his head from side to side (his only movement!), he availed himself of technology to activate switches by blowing into narrow tubes, thus enabling him to use the phone, television, recorded books, and so on. He did *not* become depressed or self-pitying, but occupied his mind with ways to go on living as full a life as possible.

Today, at age seventy-five, Proctor goes to the office every day, where he is president of his company. He maintains an active correspondence with friends and business associates. Within the last couple of years, he has designed, patented, and begun to manufacture a "load extender," a kind of heavy trailer to make earth-moving trucks more efficient. He dubbed it "The Proc." He is an avid reader, enjoys playing bridge, has continued an active social life, and travels to a summer home in Wisconsin.

His wife had remained loving, loyal, and supportive. But a few years ago she died of cancer, leaving Proctor on his own —except for his friends, family, and helpers. Then, in November 1991—seventy-five years of age and paralyzed from the neck down—he remarried! To avoid local publicity in Wichita, he and Betty, a lively widow near his age, eloped!

The point here is not Proctor's incredible victory over almost total disability, but rather, that he has chosen to continue to work, and that in doing so, to make the most of his life. The twinkle in his eyes and his warm smile exude a genuine zest for living each day to the fullest.

You need only look around you to see many people in their seventies, eighties, and nineties who are filled with this kind of joy, have rich friendships, and are excited about their work. Too busy to talk about their aches and pains, they are *involved* people, looking outward, rather than inward. They are following their bliss— an attainable goal for anyone who carefully employs creative life planning.

5

You Too Can Be a Leader

Joy can be real only if people look upon their lives as a service, and have a definite object in life outside of themselves and their personal happiness.

—Leo Tolstoy

Example is not the main thing in influencing others. It is the only thing.

—Albert Schweitzer

We have seen that work is the essential ingredient in a happy, fulfilling and healthy third half of your life. But lest you think that some kind of make-work is sufficient, lest you think that the purpose of life is to keep busy, consider this: the third half is the ideal, optimum time to assume a position of *leadership,* not only for your own sake but for the sake of society.

You are probably more qualified for leadership than you realize. You have had a decent education. You have had a successful full-time career. You are mature, with experience, judgement, and skills in human relationships—and, now, you have the freedom and flexibility to choose how you want to put these qualities to work.

THE SERVANT AS LEADER

The job you had in the second half of life is not particularly relevant. Your job title may or may not have been supervisor, manager, or executive. It doesn't matter, because titles are given to you by your employer. A leader is given that role by those who turn to him or her for help, advice, encouragement, and guidance.

Robert Greenleaf, formerly of AT&T, who founded the practice of organization and executive development, sets forth in his *Servant as Leader* the thesis that effective leadership comes from those who think of themselves first as a servant and second as a leader. If it is the reverse, the individual is usually motivated by a power drive geared to material gain, and in the long run his effectiveness is diminished. The effective leader, on the other hand, is *chosen* by those he serves.

BRUCE

Bruce spent his working life with a major international corporation, rising during thirty-three years to a middle-management position. When he was fifty-three, his company moved to another part of the country. He was given the choice of making the move or taking early retirement. He chose the latter, and felt immensely grateful that he was able, at that late age, to find a comparable position in another firm in the same field.

In his personal life, Bruce had served in various volunteer capacities for a very large non-profit organization devoted to helping others, and eventually became a national trustee. When he was fifty-seven, secure and happy in his corporate job, he was approached with the invitation to become the worldwide leader of the non-profit organization in a highly-paid position that was "full time and then some."

"I was stunned," says Bruce. "Such a possibility had never occurred to me in my wildest moments." He was awed by the challenge of leadership. He accepted the offer and spent the next twelve-plus years managing the large enterprise, presiding at world conventions with over fifty thousand attendees, and traveling all over the United States, Canada, and other parts of the world in the service of others. "The most wonderful experience anyone could ever have," is the way he describes it.

At age seventy, convinced that challenging work was the answer to staying sharp and healthy, Bruce resigned from his leadership position to start still another thriving career requiring another lifelong skill he had yet to use!

ATTRIBUTES OF A LEADER

Greenleaf characterizes an effective leader as one who:

· Knows the goal and can articulate it; sees the overarching purpose and excites others to strive to accomplish it.
· Takes initiative; is willing to risk failure, saying, in effect, 'Follow me. I will go first'—even when the course is uncertain.
· Listens long and well, building loyalty and strength in others just by paying attention to what they think.
· Expresses him or herself well.
· Understands the importance of withdrawing as necessary for refreshment and self-renewal.

Finally, Greenleaf says, the effective leader should be simultaneously an interpreter of history, an analyst of the current situation, and a prophet of the future.

If the description sounds daunting, remember that all these qualities can be learned. A former chief executive officer of a major corporation and superb business leader admits in his memoirs, "I spent sixteen years in school earning a Ph.D. in physical chemistry, but not one hour in preparation for being a CEO. When they thrust on me the job of running this huge company, it was a case of learning on the job."

Not all of us are physical chemists, but all of us are good at something. In the second half of life, you may have been with government, private industry, or other institutions. You may have been a technician, a professional, or a manager. Your career may have been in the arts or small business or raising a family and operating a household. Whatever you did, you have the background for leadership—which is sorely needed in today's society.

YOU TOO CAN BE A LEADER

MARY

A typical woman of the silent generation, Mary was married in her early twenties, made a home she was proud of, raised three children, and planted a beautiful garden—all of which she loved doing. When her children "flew the nest," she got a job for ten years as career counselor in a personnel agency. Now in the third half of life, she is a devoted and active grandmother, but she has also notified her husband and children that she intends to "do her thing"—preferably in some way that makes the world a better place.

Today she is being paid to run her town's ambitious and successful municipal beautification program. This job requires that she use many of the attributes of leadership described by Greenleaf. She is a good communicator and writer, a talent she has sharpened. However, she says her most helpful skills are those she practiced as a homemaker: "Managing a hundred things all at once." This, along with her knowledge of plants and gardening, which she acquired at the same time, are the cornerstones of her present leadership job. Mary is almost bursting with enthusiasm and excitement just talking about it, and the town has never looked as beautiful.

PAUL

Paul is now about six years into the third half of his life. He has a wife, four grown children and a passel of grandchildren. He and his family spend part of the winter skiing in Utah and summers on Nantucket Island, where they enjoy tennis and sailing. Having spent a long career as an officer for a major bank, which took him to Africa, Asia and the Middle East, he had carefully put away savings and was financially secure to make choices in his retirement.

In addition to his many active interests, he wanted to do something entirely new, something to help other people. Paul's answer was to become a consultant for the International Executive Service Corps (IESC), a private agency dedicated to matching retired executives with projects in third world countries. The IESC offers no salary, but does cover expenses for consultant and spouse. Paul was sent to Kenya for three months to help a small finance company establish a credit process. He taught them how to set up accounts and how to get paid. He also wrote a credit manual for them. Another time, he went to Trinidad and Tobago for six weeks, where he held a seminar for the management of a company that was in trouble. These assignments, together with occasionally consulting for banks and finance companies at home, average out to about a week a month—just the right amount of time, as far as he is concerned, to allow him to manage his own affairs, enjoy sports, and be with his family.

Paul observes, "The more you get involved in something, the more you enjoy it. I like being a teacher and mentor to managements that need what I have to offer. What could be better than doing it on paid trips to interesting places. I'll tell you one thing for sure: I get more out of each experience than the recipients do."

Public service in government is an arena in which the wisdom and experience of maturity is often a definite asset. President Herbert Hoover's career lasted until his death at ninety. Dwight Eisenhower was active in public service until he was seventy-seven. Ronald Reagan became president at age seventy-two and stayed in office until he was eighty. These men were elected to the highest leadership of the nation because they were vibrantly alive, active, and involved in their third half of life. But even more important to us here, they remained vibrant because they had a leadership role to fill every day.

You needn't aspire to the presidency to engage in helping society in new ways. Alumni of the Princeton University class of 1955 in 1989 founded the Center for Civic Leadership. Some of the people involved in this endeavor are still active in their full-time careers; others are in the third half of life. They are dedicated to addressing some of the major problems in our society today. One example: the Character Education Program, which brings together educators and interested citizens to revive the teaching of ethics and values in the American school system. The people of the Center for Civic Leadership are not trying to do the job themselves, but rather to provide the *leadership.* Hundreds of people have found the Center an effective new mechanism through which to channel their experience, capabilities, and commitment to make a difference in the world.

In 1990, *The Wall Street Journal* reported on a Roper survey that asked people to name "the most important thing" in their lives. Astonishingly, forty-one percent of the adult Americans surveyed put leisure ahead of work. A much lower percentage voted for work. Among college students, it was even higher—forty-seven percent considered leisure paramount, while thirty percent favored work. However, for executives, work came first. These people confessed that even while doing leisure activities, they thought about their jobs, which already claimed sixty to seventy hours per week. This brings to mind the potential workaholic in all of us when we're involved in a job that brings us satisfaction.

Executives are leaders. By the time we reach the third half of life, there is no reason why we can't all be leaders. Because by this time in life, we are all expert at something. We have something we're good at that we can pass on to others. Putting ourselves on the line, being involved, and taking responsibility, is what life is all about. That is what ultimately creates happiness. So the third half of life is the time when the executive in us should come forth in a unique and special way.

It should be emphasized that your project need not be a "big deal." Find your niche, the small place where you can leverage your talents and energy. You needn't strive to be a hero; you just need to feel good about making good things happen.

Historian and philosopher Will Durant suggests that historically leaders have been people with a "high sense of purpose." That's the main thing you need to have. If you are aware of your knowledge, skills, and experience, and apply those attributes to a strong sense of purpose in your life, there will be no stopping you! Better yet, in the third half of life you have the priceless freedom and flexibility to choose the direction your purpose will take.

JAMES A. LINEN

President of Time Inc., James Linen was a nationally known leader in the publishing business. In his fifties, he was forced to resign because of a paralyzing stroke that left him confined to a wheelchair. However, his mind was sharp as ever, and he would not give in nor give up on the things in life that were important to him. He was strongly supported by his wife and family, who urged him to keep active.

So, from his wheelchair, he continued to be in demand to consult with international businesses and foreign governments. He served on the U.S.-Japan Foundation, the Urban League, and the American Red Cross. His schedule required him to travel abroad at least three times a year, which he did with the aid of a companion.

James Linen's physical power had been taken from him. But he continued to *lead* because, as Greenleaf pointed out, he was selected to do so by those he served.

JAMES H. COLEMAN

Journalism graduate Jim Coleman was working for a wire service in New York City when World War II broke out. Labeled 4-F because of poor eyesight, he joined the Office of War Information, which sent him to Australia. There he married an Australian woman and has remained "down under" ever since. He became the successful publisher of a popular magazine, several trade publications, and books. After four decades, at age seventy, he sold his business, continuing as a consultant while he looked around for something else to do.

On his annual trips to America, Coleman was impressed with *Modern Maturity,* the magazine for members of AARP, and thought there might be a market for that kind of periodical in Australia. Investigating further, he found there was no Australian organization comparable to AARP. So in his mid-seventies, he became the founder, organizer, and leader of that kind of movement, as well as the publisher of its magazine. He is busier and more prominent than ever in the affairs of his adopted land.

If you in the third half of life are concerned for the world in which your children and grandchildren will be living—as many of us are—take comfort in the realization that this is the ideal, optimum time in your life to do something about it. If *all* of us became willing to assume leadership for a better society, we could make an enormous difference. As Margaret Mead once said, "Never doubt that a small group of thoughtful, committed people can change the world. Indeed, it is the only thing that ever has."

HOW TO
MAKE IT HAPPEN

In these chapters, based on The Third Half of Life Seminar (See Appendix), you will learn the practical aspects of planning for and creating a dynamic and enjoyable future. We've included many examples and checklists of questions and issues that you need to address.

By focusing on how to manage the change from your full-time career to the third half of life, this section will help you set priorities for planning ahead. Start by explicitly clarifying just who you are, and how you plan to cultivate future relationships with family and friends.

Then, look beyond your personal self to the world around you. What turns you on? How can you turn a lifetime of experiences into the experience of a lifetime? Business, professional activities, civic leadership, or some combination?

Next, you need to take a look at your financial picture, followed by your learning and leisure interests. In your third half you will have the freedom and flexibility to improve the balance in your life. You also should consider where you will want to live. Lastly, you will want to develop a prudent approach to managing your health.

In this section, you will meet people already satisfied and productive in their third half—further proof that the best really is yet to come!

6

Getting Started

Enough of this theorizing. By now we hope you're interested in making the most of your third half of life. So when do you begin?

Now. Don't wait another day. If you are over fifty-five, you are already late. The old truism gets truer every day as you get older, "Today *is* the first day of the rest of your life."

How do you get started? Begin with your attitude toward change.

CHANGE IS INEVITABLE—AND TOUGH

Most of us hate change and we resist it. We prefer the known, safe, and predictable. Back in 1970, Alvin Toffler in his best-seller, *Future Shock,* warned us that the sudden, major changes taking place at an accelerating speed would cause people shattering stress and disorientation. He called this sickness "the disease of change." Retirement is that kind of change. So to avoid the discomfort of planning for it, we avoid facing the reality of it.

But change is as inevitable as spring becoming summer and summer fading into fall. Instead of fighting it, we need to embrace it with optimism and enthusiasm. To do this, it is helpful to anticipate change and plan for it. For example, our bodies are going to change in the third half of life. You probably won't be able to do some sports you used to enjoy. (Though not necessarily—remember Loren in chapter 1.) You may have aches and pains or even illness. But if you begin early enough with good health habits (no smoking, no boozing), proper exercise and proper nutrition, there's no reason you can't have good health until the day you die. (More on this in chapter 13.)

Besides the changes that are going to happen whether you like them or not, you also might think about changes you would *like* to make. Here are some tips from United Technologies.

> *Oscar Wilde said, "Consistency is the last refuge of the unimaginative." So stop getting up at 6:05. Walk a mile at dawn. Find a new way to drive to work. Switch chores with your spouse next Saturday. Buy a wok. Study wildflowers. Stay up alone all night. Read to the blind. Start counting brown-eyed blonds. Subscribe to an out-of-town paper. Don't write to your congressman, take a whole scout troop to see him. Learn to speak Italian. Teach some kid the things you do best. Listen to two hours of uninterrupted Mozart. Take up aerobic dancing. Leap out of that rut. Savor life. Remember, we only pass this way once.*

And before retirement is upon you, begin to get the set of your mind in order (see chapter 3). Face the fact that the real quality of your life—at *any* stage, but especially the third half—is up to you. You can—and must—take responsibility for yourself.

TRANSLATING YOUR PAST INTO YOUR FUTURE

Your objective is to use your accumulated wisdom, experience, and yearnings to create a life pattern that will combine work, learning, leisure, and service to others in ways that will be satisfying and fulfilling to you.

Let's look at how three people successfully made the change from the second half of life to the third.

TED

Ted worked for the same company for twenty-five years, the last ten in the same job, so he was becoming stale. During that period, his longtime marriage ended in divorce, contributing to his dissatisfaction with life. Then his company offered him a "golden handshake" to retire early, giving him two months to decide. "I had never given a thought to the future and had no idea what I would do," admits Ted. "I accepted the offer with the attitude, 'What the hell, I have nothing to lose.'"

But it turned out he had a lot to lose. He lost his identity, because his job had defined who he was. And he lost his social life, which had consisted almost completely of his associates and business friends. Consequently, he *felt* lost. After a few months of trying to distract himself with museum visits and plays, he experienced depression and a lack of confidence. He angrily blamed the company for rushing him into such an unhappy decision.

Fortunately, Ted sought counseling. In the process, he remembered how he had once loved carpentry. At the urging of his counselor, he contacted town authorities regarding some community needs where he might help. As a result, today he has a small home remodeling business, and as much work as he cares to do. He finds it most rewarding. He also works part time for the Public Works Department of his town and volunteers at the community center. As he turned his focus from his former company to the outside world, he picked up old friendships and developed new ones. He feels good about himself again.

KARL

In common with hundreds of other CPAs working for accounting firms, Karl, who was with a firm in the midwest, knew he would have to "retire" at age sixty. He also knew he wanted to keep going in a full-time job. So when the time came, he moved over to manage the back-office operations of one of his financial services clients.

Karl's wife, Erica, was devoted to a number of volunteer interests that she began pursuing after their children were grown.

A couple of years into his new job, Karl saw that the challenge of restructuring the back office would be gone, and his heavy, inflexible work schedule was beginning to be a burden.

But he liked working and appreciated the extra income. For her part, Erica wanted more time to travel and to see more of their grandchildren. They weren't sure what to do.

At this juncture, they took part in our life planning seminar. During those three days, they got in touch with old, unrealized dreams and interests. They decided what they wanted, where to start, and left with definite plans.

Today, Karl works thirty-five weeks a year—half as a paid consultant to financial services firms with back-office problems, half as the volunteer regional head of a "mentoring" program for inner city grade school children. Erica is continuing her community interests, and, with Karl, spends one day a week as a mentor. The other seventeen weeks of the year, they take bicycle trips with groups of their general age as well as doing more conventional travel; they visit their grandchildren, and they have taken up golf. They have even rekindled friendships left behind in the rush of the second half of life. In short, they are thoroughly enjoying themselves.

IDA DAVIDOFF

At eighty-seven, Dr. Ida Davidoff is an inspirational example of older growing and making the most of the third half of her life. Indeed, she describes herself as a pioneer in developing this concept.

When Ida was fifty-five, with her children fast growing up, she began to experience the empty nest syndrome. She decided to do something about it. "Mind you," she says, "in those days, anyone over forty-five was 'over the hill,' and society was simply unaccustomed to a middle-aged, married female becoming a career woman." Nevertheless, using her twenty-odd years of experience as a wife and mother as her only qualification, she applied and was accepted at Columbia University to study psychology and education. At age fifty-eight, she received a doctoral degree in education.

Dr. Davidoff started a successful marriage and family counseling practice, which turned out to be part of the beginning of family therapy as it is known today. Countless individuals, couples, and families regard her with deep gratitude and love because of the guidance and support she gave them when they needed it.

Now in her late eighties, she is still practicing! But Dr. Davidoff is again pioneering a new cause: changing the stereotype of aging. Using herself as a prime example of how old age can be different, she describes her steadfast fight against "the myth of the little old, bent-over lady." In an interview with *The New York Times* in April 1991, she shared ideas for not feeling old. At eighty-three, after hearing that women's voices deteriorate with age, she started singing lessons. At eighty-seven, she still plays the piano; she does duets with a friend for an hour each week. "It's so exhilarating," she enthuses, "we hug each other at the end." Three times a week her physical trainer comes to her house. What kind of exercise does she do? "Why, I pump iron." She swims daily, and is still dieting, though she loves to cook. (Last year she had her kitchen renovated.)

"We don't simply grow old," Ida declares. "We become old from not growing." She advises, "Live as if you're going to live forever or die tomorrow." She is now writing a book to be titled *Age: A Work of Art,* using herself as Exhibit A.

What can we learn from these three cases? Ted admittedly "had never given a thought to the future," with nearly disastrous results. His turning point came when he sought professional help, which prompted him to plan a fulfilling third half. Karl made the opposite error. Wisely knowing he wanted to continue working, he opted for what turned out to be an extension of his second half. He also failed to consider his wife's needs. Together, they were able to make a *transition* to their third half which combined Karl's desire to continue working (but on a reduced schedule) with their mutual interest in helping others and their common recreational and family activities. When Dr. Davidoff saw the inevitability of being out of her parenting job soon, she didn't wring her hands and feel sorry for herself. She faced the reality of the change and did something about it. Although devoted to her husband and family, she knew she couldn't lean on them for happiness and wanted more out of life. Incidentally, she says her husband and children supported her all the way.

Meet another successful example.

THOMAS WATSON

The "retired" CEO of IBM and former ambassador to the Soviet Union is anything but your run-of-the-mill retiree and his approach to life at eighty is illuminating. Thomas Watson, Jr., took over the reins of IBM from his father, the founder of the company, when he was forty-four. When he resigned fifteen years later after a heart attack, IBM was a $7.5 billion business. And at age fifty-nine, he had his whole third half of life ahead of him.

An avid amateur pilot since he flew in World War II, Watson still flies his own Lear jet. (He parks the plane outside the nearby Westchester County Airport because he thinks the hangar rent is too high!) He sails his seventy-five-foot yacht to remote corners of the world. He attempted to climb the Matterhorn at age sixty-five, and was surprised and disappointed that he didn't make it to the top. He's a devoted family man, married over fifty years, with six children and fifteen grandchildren. At age seventy-eight, he authored a humble and candid book, *Father, Son & Co.: My Life at IBM and Beyond*, which enjoyed a long run on *The New York Times* "Best Sellers" list.

Speaking of his "strategy in life," Tom says, "you might have a stroke or whatever, but if you have an ambition in front of you, it gives you an incentive to keep yourself in physical shape. Always keep something ahead of you that's vigorous and challenging."

Now that you've had a chance to see how other people handle change, why not test your own attitudes. Honestly examine your thoughts and feelings—no one but you need ever see your private notebook. So get a pen and jot down your responses to the following questions.

QUESTIONS TO GET YOU STARTED

- Am I prepared for major changes in my future? Do I acknowledge that the switch from second half to third half is probably going to mean some important changes? Do I accept the fact that by their very nature, changes, especially major ones such as retirement from a long career, can produce stress and I need to prepare myself?
- Do I see myself as responsible for the quality of my life, knowing I can't depend on anyone else for my happiness?
- With my new promise of freedom and flexibility, what sort of balance of learning, work, and leisure appears most attractive and healthy to me? Am I thinking about having some of each?
- What projects do I foresee enjoying in my future years? Are they long-term, or short-term? Will society benefit, directly or indirectly?
- Do I really accept that potentially a whole third of my life is ahead, and that not only *can* I think that way, I *need* to? Have I pictured what a thirty-year vacation would be like? Would I be willing to consider investing some of my valuable time, even money (*not* "grocery" money), in order to avoid such a fate?
- Am I excited about what my activities and involvements may be? Do they contain some challenges? Are they venturesome with some risk involved? Would they be fun for me? Are there people in my network who could give me further ideas about contacts I can make now to get started?

7

Who Are You?

A prerequisite to planning for a third half of life filled with more fun and satisfaction than you have ever dreamed is to stand back and take a look at yourself and your life to date. Who are you? Take an inventory of your accomplishments and capabilities. What are your values and interests? Finally, look inside yourself and discover your unfulfilled dreams. When you have done these things, you will have the insight necessary to plan a satisfying life ahead.

SIGNIFICANT EVENTS IN YOUR LIFE

First of all, in your notebook, make a chart of the most important experiences and achievements in your life. Note the year and your age at the time of each event. Identify at least a dozen that have played a significant role in shaping your life. Be sure to include both positive and negative events—ones that were satisfying and enjoyable, as well as experiences that might have seemed traumatic at the time, but which you now can see were life-changing, ultimately positive episodes. Next, mark the ones that involved accomplishments and contributions through work, family or community service.

YOUR ACCOMPLISHMENTS

These past achievements are the first building blocks in erecting the structure for your future. Now, make a list of at least four of these accomplishments that make you particularly proud. Be honest, but don't be too humble. Perhaps you turned a moribund company around and made it prosper. Or raised a family—definitely a major accomplishment! Maybe you caught a winning touchdown, or painted a memorable picture. Here are some examples:

- A former advertising executive rates running a mission on skid row in downtown Los Angeles as his greatest accomplishment.
- Tom Watson, Jr., who helped IBM become one of the world's greatest companies, lists among his major accomplishments climbing Mount Blanc at age twelve and ferrying lend-lease planes across Siberia during World War II.
- A senator who guided some of the nation's most important legislation into law states unequivocally that his greatest accomplishment was to recover from alcoholism.

After you have listed your accomplishments, review each one by asking yourself: What challenges did I face? How did I overcome the obstacles? Which of my capabilities did I apply, and how? What did I most enjoy? You may gain some clues about yourself, what you are best at and what you enjoy doing most.

YOUR VALUES

Your personal values are those things that truly matter to you, the principles you *really* believe in, the essential elements of who you are. Although they have been influenced by your parents, peers, and friends and by your education, career, and worklife, they are just you. There are no right or wrong answers.

To discover which values are most important to you, use your notebook. Be clear with yourself. Prioritizing your values into these five catagories will make this step easier:

Your personal world
What do you find necessary to be truly comfortable: Good health? Law and order? Freedom? Excitement? Independence? Pleasant surroundings? Make your own list.

BEATING THE AGE GAME

Qualities in yourself and others

Which ones make all the difference in your feeling good about yourself or in your liking another person? Is it being intelligent? Efficient? Sexually attractive? Responsible? Active? Conventional? Considerate? Honest? For instance, a friend of ours holds that "the most important thing in *any* person is to have a sense of humor and not take themselves too seriously." Think about your own favorite people. What qualities do they have that make you like them?

Your personal relationships

What kinds of relationships are most important to you: A few close friends or a wide circle of people? Intimacy? Fun? Mutual interests? A widower friend of ours seeks out women who share his interest in music and art.

Someone with whom you can play tennis or fish or ride horseback? Buddies of your same gender, or contacts with the opposite sex that add a spark? David Brown cautions men retirees against hanging out with their cronies; instead he advises, go to lunch regularly with women friends. There is nothing like the opposite sex to make you spruce up and converse brightly. (And maybe we should remind you ladies that in this new and liberal world today, you can take the initiative and do the same thing!)

The world out there

Beyond your personal world, what issues concern you deeply: The drug problem? Women's rights? Gun control? An improved educational system? Effective local government? Ecology? For instance we know of a woman who is knowledgeable in horitculture who's mounted a one-woman crusade against knapweed, a blight that threatens western states.

Your worklife

What are the most essential aspects of your enjoyment in your work: Financial reward? Challenge? Making a difference in the world? Pleasant surroundings? People you meet? One man in his seventies says, "The best thing about my job is feeling needed."

After you've made your list for each of the five value categories, identify the *three most important* to you in each category. These are the values you will want to honor in your future no matter what.

YOUR INTERESTS

What turns you on? How would you like to spend your time if you could? Some interests are obvious, but as you move from the second half to the third half of life, you may find that activities which formerly enthralled you are no longer exciting.

For example, the wife of a business leader who spent some time living abroad says, "We entertained a lot, and being 'the hostess with the mostest' was my main interest, plus feeling I had to be the president of every women's club in sight. Now I don't care if I ever give another big party and I realize I don't really enjoy running meetings. My biggest interest these days is getting everyone in our big, wonderful family—four generations of them—to write his or her own brief autobiography, their memories, et cetera. I'm going to collect them, edit them, have them printed in book form, and then give a copy to each member of the family. I'm also doing a regular genealogy, running down photos of our forebears where possible. Later I plan to organize a big reunion of the whole clan—maybe fifty or a hundred people—which has never been done. I estimate the whole project will take four or five years." Her eyes sparkle as she talks about it.

There may even be an interest from your youth that got left behind and would be fun to pick up again. So get your notebook out again, and just as you did with your values, divide your interests—this time into three categories:

Your leisure interests
In your third half of life, you will have time just to enjoy yourself, to do things you've always wanted to do but never had the chance. What would you love to do: Amateur theater? Fishing? Hiking? Sports? Gardening? Make your own list.

- One man took up chess, and found it absorbing. He plays for fun with friends and competes with younger opponents—sometimes by long-distance phone!
- A woman loved dogs as a youngster, but never had one in her second half; now she raises Bernese mountain dogs.
- Malcolm Forbes took up motorcycling and hot-air ballooning late in life.

- Howard Turtle, Sunday editor of the *Kansas City Star,* had put himself through college by playing trumpet in a dance band. He knew he still "had the lip," so after enduring a couple of years of boredom in retirement, he picked up his instrument again. Now in his eighties, he plays twice a week with a Dixieland band and even sits in with other professional groups when he and his wife travel. It is a lifesaving and consuming interest for him, and gives pleasure to others as well.
- The father of a friend of ours who loves acting is spreading lots of pleasure by presenting monologues to friends, organizations —anyone he can find.

Your learning interests

At least a dozen times in your busiest years you've probably thought, "I wish I could go back to school and take a course in that." Or, "I'd sure like to know more about the other." The years ahead give you that opportunity. Learning is not only fun in itself, but it can open doors to new and fascinating avenues of work. What might you like to learn: History? Perhaps a science you missed, such as astronomy or comparative religion? Art? Or a sport such as skiing or rowing?

- One woman we know took a painting course and became so good that she has exhibited widely and has had one-woman shows.
- One man had wanted to learn to play the drums as a kid. Now he has realized that ambition, and his wife is still adjusting!
- One ambitious widow took a course in archeology and has gone on a number of digs in exotic places.
- Another man, a Civil War buff, has taken a number of history courses on the subject and has visited most of the battlefields.

Your work interests

If your main work interest is the career you followed in the second half of your life, that's fine. But bear in mind, this is your chance to choose something entirely new. And remember that whatever you choose can be part time or full time, paid or volunteer, entrepreneurial or academic. Make a list of work-life possibilities that fit *your* interests. The categories are myriad. For example: interior decorating, real estate appraising, fund raising, landscape design, investment banking, aiding in a hospital, sculpting, innkeeping, and writing.

BILL

With a degree in chemical engineering, Bill went to work for a large corporation. In his thirties, he jumped ship to start his own specialized and lucrative plastics manufacturing company. When at age fifty-seven he sold it, he was fixed for life. He and his wife moved to Florida, where he was immediately restless to work again.

Sensing a need and an opportunity, he purchased a large tract of land and built a golf course, which he then managed for several years as a club. However, when he was building the course, the price he had to pay for trees and shrubs impressed upon him the notion that there must be a lot of profit in the nursery business. Starting from scratch, he studied everything he could find out about tropical plants and how to grow them commercially. When he became an expert in this new area of interest, he sold the golf course and opened a nursery. Today, almost twenty years later, he has an inventory of thousands of plants, employs a team of workers, and has a thriving business up and down Florida's east coast.

In choosing the kind of work for your third half of life, you will be happiest if you can combine what you are good at with what you really enjoy doing. The two are not necessarily the same. Rate yourself on both counts with regard to these aspects of your worklife. Managing your own time? Working alone? Solving organizational problems? Being on a small team? Networking with others? For instance, you might think you would like to write a book in your retirement. This requires not only competency in writing plus ability to operate a computer or word processor, but it is also a loner's profession. If you don't enjoy being alone very much, writing is not for you.

Go back through your lists and check your top three priorities in each category of interest. Now compare these with your highest personal values from the previous section. Do they seem to jibe? They should, if you are to have a happy and fulfilling third half.

YOUR CAPABILITIES

In addition to your values and your interests, you should assess your capabilities—your innate talents, acquired skills, and demonstrated competencies. Your capabilities will greatly influence how you spend the learning, work, and leisure hours that lie ahead. There are two kinds of capabilities: your "soft" interpersonal capabilities, and your "hard" technical capabilities. Let's look at each.

Soft interpersonal capabilities are most often used in communications, administration, and relationships. For example, negotiating, counseling, planning, running a meeting, and public speaking. You probably have more of these kinds of skills than you realize. So in making your list, don't be modest. Are you good at conceptualizing? Presenting information? Counseling and advising? Planning? Delegating? Analyzing? Writing and editing?

Hard technical capabilities are those skills and areas of knowledge that you learned either in school or from experience. Examples include teaching, managing, selling, accounting, carpentry, architecture, and cooking.

We know two men—one, a former corporate executive and the other, a retired cardiologist—who have had a lifelong, passionate interest in cooking. In both cases, cooking would be high on their interest and capability lists. Having plenty of time to prepare gourmet meals and exotic dishes is one of the great rewards of their third half of life.

On the other hand, many silent generation housewives and mothers who come to us feel, mistakenly, that they lack hard capabilities and experience. Wrong! If you are one of these women, you have a vast array of experience and skills that have been honed and tested daily (without time off for weekends!) for decades. Among other things, you have been a facilities manager, events manager, chef, mediator, caterer, nurse, and transportation coordinator. And this is only the beginning of your list of capabilities. Don't underestimate yourself.

Your own capabilities may apply in unexpected ways. When one of our clients came up with an inadequate list, we tried to probe deeper. When we asked if he had education or experience in public relations, he just snorted scornfully and replied, "None at all. I don't know a thing about public relations, and I don't want to!" But when we pointed out that public relations embraced such specific functions as writing, editing, graphic design, media relations, running events, and production of printed materials, his face lit up. "I used to be an estimator in a printing plant," he said. "I know *all* about production and scheduling." It turned out that a public relations agency headquartered near his home needed exactly that expertise on a part-time basis, and age was no barrier. It was a happy "marriage" for both.

Identify four or five of your soft capabilities and two or three of your hard capabilities. Now, relate the skills you enjoy most with your list of interests. Do some go together? For example, an interest in literacy could go with capabilities in teaching, tutoring or counseling. An interest in counseling could go with skills in finance or accounting. An interest in almost any cause or organization could go with capabilities in managing, planning, operating a computer, writing or public speaking.

As you see, by following these logical steps you are simultaneously broadening your horizon of opportunities and also zeroing in on your options. Who are you? You are a unique individual with your own set of values, your own interests, your special capabilities, and your impressive accomplishments. If you have diligently followed the suggestions above, you should be aware that you are qualified in ways you may not have realized. In the chapter that follows, we will move from self-awareness to awareness of your relationships with others. But first, take time to make sure you are truly in touch with who you are.

QUESTIONS TO DISCOVER THE TOTAL YOU

The Inner You:

- What are your personal qualities—the parts of yourself that are primarily intrinsic? Are you enthusiastic? Do you dislike being wrong? Do you like structure? Do you have high energy? Do you

get along well with people? Are you shy? Aggressive? Controlling? Passive?
- What are your strong points? What qualities help you achieve what you want—despite barriers that get in the way. For example, are you willing to try? Are you a hard worker? Do you have a positive attitude? Good health? Humility?
- What are your values? What do you expect of yourself? Of others? Do you like being alone? Do you need structure? Freedom? Independence?
- What are the things that could hold you back from accomplishing your goals? For example: Are you a procrastinator? Are you lazy? Afraid of failure? Unsure about how to start? Think about the people who might help you to overcome such barriers.

The Outer You:

- What activities do you enjoy doing?
- What are the family activities you look forward to most?
- What do you like most about the world outdoors?
- What are the artistic, creative aspects of your life?
- What kinds of things do you most enjoy doing for others?
- What do you know that you'd enjoy teaching others?
- If you had a completely free year, what would you do?

8

The People
In Your Life

We mark with light in the memory the few interviews we have had, in the dreary years of routine and sin, with souls that made our souls wiser; that spoke what we thought; that told us what we knew; that gave us leave to be what we inly were.

— Ralph Waldo Emerson

Emerson has captured the precious value of certain rare people in our lives. He conveys the beauty of a wonderful relationship with such people. People are vital to the quality of our existence all through our lives. However, the kinds and numbers of relationships we have change with the stages we are in. For example, adults with no children at home usually have more time for deep friendships than when they were parents with kids growing up.

One bonus of the third half of life is having the time and energy to broaden and deepen your personal connections. You will have more space in your life; fill some of it with loving and being loved in return.

However, these blessings do not come automatically, nor are they easy to attain. You will need a generous measure of self-awareness, sensitivity to the needs of others, and willingness to work at your relationships.

TRANSITION TIME

The end of your full-time career life brings an abrupt cutoff from your business associates. The people with whom you worked, lunched, and interacted are suddenly no longer there. When, at your retirement banquet, the boss says, "We'll be calling frequently on Fred here for his advice and counsel," don't you believe it. When he adds, "We'll miss you, Fred, and look forward to seeing you often," he's just being nice. Recall for a moment your own feelings when the old boys dropped into the office to see you. Sure, you were glad to see them and asked how they were doing, but weren't you also vaguely uncomfortable? You were busy with other matters, and there wasn't much more to say. Secretly, you hoped they wouldn't hang around till lunchtime.

DREW

Drew was the president and CEO of a large company in the retailing field. He was good at his job and loved it—the title, the prestige, the perks, the spectacular office overlooking the Hudson River. His travels and social life were intertwined with those of the principals of the firm. When his retirement day came, he was honored and feted.

Three years later, his wife Helen says bitterly, "Since that day, Drew hasn't heard one word from anyone in that whole organization. It's as if we've dropped off the face of the earth." She continues with hurt in her voice, "We put the present CEO in. We entertained him and his wife again and again. After Drew stepped down, they haven't contacted us even once . . ."

Faced with such abrupt cessation of business relationships, some men are tempted to isolate themselves. They draw into their shells or develop an unhealthy, clinging dependency on spouses or children, rather than allow themselves to become vulnerable by trying new things. Drew and Helen simply didn't realize that too often in the corporate world, when you're out, you're out. Gone is forgotten.

Fortunately, Drew, who has a happy, optimistic disposition, almost immediately filled his life with several directorships on the boards of companies and volunteer organizations and is president of his condominium association. He enjoys the added leisure time he now has for golf and boating. And Helen, grateful to have additional time with her husband, children and grandchildren, has had no trouble developing new friends and community activities. (It would have been better, however, if they'd known what to expect.)

At the very least, the transition from a full-time career will require reassessing who is important to you and who is not. With the former, you should concentrate on improving existing relationships; with the latter, it might be better to let the relationships lapse and seek to meet new people.

SPOUSES

First and foremost—indeed, a prerequisite to all other relationships —is your spouse. The third half of life can be either the crowning experience in a marriage relationship; or it can be disastrous, damaging or even the end of a marriage.

THE GOOD NEWS

The potential for the positive is beautifully expressed by Barbara DeFrank Lynch, associate professor of marital and family therapy and director of the Family Clinic at Southern Connecticut State College. Professor Lynch writes:

> *The last stage [of marriage], the one of genuine intimacy, makes all the rest of the work (in the earlier growth stages) worth the time and effort. This is the time of fellow travelers riding separate bikes together, still going over rough spots together and not losing each other. This is usually an older couple who have worked to gain self-respect, trust, and faith—and can extend the same privilege to the partner. They have a sense of security that comes from their shared history and the knowledge that they don't need each other—but rather, choose to be together, mutually enhancing and enhanced. They are two healthy, whole people, ready and willing to bring excitement into their relationship . . .*

> It is characterized by a genuine acceptance of self and mate, and is accompanied by a relinquishing of fantasies in favor of reality . . . Arguments are based on genuine differences; fights are for change. There is a win-win quality that follows creative problem solving and innovative ways of arguing . . . The couple that views all the issues as challenges to be met, rather than seeing them as insurmountable problems that keep them stuck, have the ability to discover the pot of gold at the end of the rainbow.

THE BAD NEWS

On the negative side, in an article from *The New York Times,* Gary Lee, gerontologist and professor of sociology at the University of Florida, says flatly, "Retirement has no beneficial effects on the quality of marriages among older people." He has found that most major problems occur when the husband retires but the wife continues to work. He supports our premise that preretirement planning will help strengthen relationships and avoid these problems, and that continued work life is vital. In a related *Times* article, another gerontologist, Patricia Keegan, reports her research shows the most common problems retired couples face are increased amount of time together, divergent interests, reduced sexual intimacy, less income, and deteriorating health.

A husband, when asked what he was doing in retirement, replied, "I've gotten into the 'honeydew' business." "What's that?" inquired his friend. He replied, "Honey, do this" and "Honey, do that." A wife, when asked how retirement life suited her, answered, "I have twice as much husband and half as much money."

Careful and realistic planning can help avoid *all* the problem areas cited by Dr. Keegan.

SARAH and PHIL

Sarah and Phil are a typical silent generation couple, married thirty-five years with three children. Phil, a lawyer with a large company, after twenty-five years was promoted to a position that necessitated their moving to a new part of the country and his being away a lot. With their children having gone,

Sarah was lonely in the new location. She had no roots and no old friends.

To cope with the long evenings, Sarah began to find solace in a few drinks. Then more drinks, which fueled her feelings of self-pity and anger with her husband. Phil felt badly, but was helpless in the face of demands on his time. When Phil was home, he found her increasingly silent and hostile. His way of handling it was avoidance—to make idle conversation and not confront what was happening.

After about a year and yet one more uncommunicative evening, Sarah packed her bags and left for her parents' home. When Phil returned from his trip, he found the house empty. There followed several months of separation, at the end of which Phil's company offered him an "early out" package. Tired, sick of the rat race, and depressed over the separation, he jumped at the offer.

Phil was tempted to pick a new wife from the attractive women he had begun to notice were available, move to some warm, sunny place, and begin again. At the same time, he felt guilty for having left Sarah alone too much, for having neglected to confront the deteriorating situation earlier, and for having failed to give her a sympathetic and receptive ear. On the other hand, he had no desire to go back to the lackluster relationship their marriage had become.

Meanwhile, Sarah, now in the comfort of her family and in contact with her children, saw that she needed help, which she got. This, in turn, led to her realization that her problem wasn't simply Phil being away. She was bored and needed new interests and new friends in her life. Remembering how she had enjoyed a job in a florist shop before her marriage, she decided to brush up on her education in floral design. With a new, warm excitement deep within her and no desire to drink, the first person she wanted to tell was Phil.

Several phone conversations followed, during which they realized they cared deeply for each other and cherished the life and family they had built. They decided to have another go at marriage. They took our life planning seminar and found they could approach the future as a big, new adventure. Over the following two years, they talked a lot, traveled a lot and "played" together a lot, sorting out ideas and plans. Sarah enrolled in an excellent course at the local botanical garden and Phil found some consulting jobs. At last report, they say they are grateful every day for their new level of mutual understanding and for being together.

ALMOST STRANGERS

Sarah and Phil's story highlights, first of all, how easy it is for couples to become almost strangers during the second half when pressures of career and family are so intense. They lose communication. Secondly, while Phil was employing his best energy and charm at work, the very characteristics that had won Sarah's heart in the first place suddenly shifted into neutral at home. Thirdly, Sarah had lapsed into a rut, making no effort to develop outside interests. Both of them had become dull. And finally, they kept their potential boat-rocking problems stuffed below the surface, putting off the task of facing up to and resolving them. This is especially common in cases where both spouses have had careers as well as family to cope with. (A book that has helped some couples we know to get new light and air into their relationship is *Getting All the Love You Want.* See the Bibliography.)

In other instances typical of the silent generation, the problem may be that the spouse, far from being in a rut, is reveling in her new-found freedom and independence. A newly retired friend of ours recalls the first time he sat at the kitchen table, in his robe, dawdling over the morning paper and a second cup of coffee. "Hey," exclaimed this startled husband when his wife appeared dressed to the teeth and headed for the door, "where are you going?" Replied she, *"You* are the one who has retired, darling; *I* haven't."

TIPS FOR A GOOD REENTRY:

We are assuming that, as is typical in the silent generation, the man is the one retiring and the woman's career base was at home. With that in mind, consider these helpful hints:

- Realize that the full-time career you are leaving has provided you with personal status, identity, and a network of friends, as well as financial security. Face up to the fact you will miss them, and plan how you will make up for their loss. One retired executive wailed, "I just can't get used to writing my own letters and making my own plane reservations!"

· Having spent decades in one mode of life, you may find it takes time to adjust to the new mode. If you are nervous about it, admit that to yourself—it's healthier. When one man retired, he found his wife's endless phone calls drove him to distraction. After years at his desk, he was glad to get away from the phone; to his wife, the phone was a link to the outside world and she loved it.

· *Promise* you won't try to reorganize her kitchen when you get home, unless she asks you to. She won't.

TIPS FOR THE SPOUSE SMOOTHING THE WAY:

· Recognize that you have regarded home as *your* turf, and that this domain will be invaded to some degree. You may lose precious privacy. Not only will your returning retiree try to rearrange your spice cabinet, but he may usurp the phone, the home computer, or the family car. To promote comfort and harmony —as well as to keep the guy out of your hair!—*you both need your own space and your own facilities.*

· Be patient with him as he makes this major adjustment in his life. After all, you have been more accustomed to making changes as your children have grown, and left. He is less experienced at handling this big transition and will need tender, loving care.

· You also will need to make some adjustments. It is imperative for each of you to continue some separate activities and keep a measure of freedom. Remember Helen, whose CEO husband had been forgotten so quickly? She confided to us, "The first two years after Drew retired, he asked every single morning, 'Well, sweetheart, what are *we* going to do today?' He followed me to the market, he even followed me around when I vacuumed. It absolutely drove me up a wall!"

TIPS FOR COUPLES:

- Discuss these matters openly, honestly, and ahead of retirement time.
- Beware of too much togetherness in your planning. Plan first for *yourself.* This is *your* life. You have your own needs. Then share your individual plans and see how they interrelate.
- Be flexible. Approach the future as a new adventure where there will be some changes in the way you have lived together. Remember, the only constant in life is change. Embrace it. Enjoy it.
- Recognize that each of you has a need for privacy; independence; security; respect; being needed; giving and loving; friends and relationships; and your own activities.
- Above all, don't fight it. Don't get uptight—and keep your sense of humor.

ALLOWING CONFLICT

Many people in the silent generation were brought up in an era when "father knew best," and a good wife was an agreeable one. Today, in most homes, such attitudes are passé. We know that married couples disagree about things—sometimes strongly. It's okay. You can disagree without being disagreeable.

Robert Coulson in his book *Fighting Fair,* which is about conflict resolution, has this to say: "Being able to disagree is healthy. A conflict-free relationship is undesirable, if not unattainable. Indeed, quarrels are stimulating. Even more important, they encourage the growth and change that lead to individual development."

THE SINGLE PERSON

Thus far we have talked about the impact of retirement on married couples. But suppose you are single. What is the impact then?

First, there are those who have been single all their lives. Their work lives have been even more important, if possible, than for married persons. They are more likely to depend on their business associates for friendship and to form routines around their business activities. Therefore, retirement may be even more traumatic. Building new relationships with outside people is vital. And continuing to work in some kind of new capacity is essential, on either a paid or volunteer basis.

OLD HANDS AT LIVING ALONE

On the other hand, single people have an advantage in that they have learned to look after themselves. Many have discovered the joys of being alone. They have developed self-reliance, a sense of self-worth, and independence. Their third half of life gives them an opportunity to expand their horizons, to take long trips they have longed for, and to try new sports or hobbies.

NEWLY WIDOWED

Then there are those who may lose a spouse on the brink of their third half. For them, singleness is a new and frightening experience. If you find yourself in this situation, you must learn to be single, to find out that being alone does not necessarily mean being lonely. You must form new routines and rhythms. Unless you are careful, it is easy to let things slide and go undone. Structuring your living is important: Make lists; keep to a schedule; plan activities that will get you out of the house and out of yourself. This is the time to use your friends. They are there for you when you need them—which is *now*.

Neglect of good nutrition is a leading cause of illness among the single. So if you don't already know how, learning to cook for yourself is an important first step. Eat regular, healthy meals. Treat yourself to your favorite dishes. Find someone who can teach you how to shop for and prepare meals—they'll be flattered you asked.

Fight depression with activity. Keep in touch with people. Have projects, stay physically active, engage regularly in a favorite activity. Keep yourself interested—and interesting to others—by reading, being a good communicator, and having interests outside yourself.

Live one day at a time. Don't dwell on past memories, and avoid projecting your fears onto the future. This is the wisdom of the ages, an integral part of most great philosophies and religions. Now is the time to practice it.

Take charge of your life and learn to take care of yourself. Be confident that living alone can be satisfying. Many have done it and, with time, have found happiness. Have faith this will happen to you.

FAMILY RELATIONS

Families are the people who love us even when we are not perfect. That's one reason why these relationships are easiest to take for granted. Take some time to look carefully at your family relations. What do you like about them? What don't you like? What would you like to change? How would you go about it?

BEING A PARENT

One of our third half of life friends, who successfully raised a brood of children, says that as she was going through her parenting era, it often seemed like a time of the "mosts"—that being a parent is the *most* natural and easy thing to do, and the *most* difficult; the *most* wonderful experience and the *most* terrible; the *most* emotional highs and the *most* lows.

It was a mass of conflicts. After getting used to the intrusion of these new beings into their lives, she and her husband had given up much of their freedom and independence, and taken on the responsibility of feeding the children, keeping them safe, and getting them educated. As parents, they had to develop a new measure of selflessness in order to *survive* (she had to *know* that her interests were totally unimportant). They had to not only get acquainted with and encourage their children's strengths, but understand and accept their weaknesses.

After doing all that, she became convinced she had been born to be a mother, and was enjoying her life completely. Then her children began to grow up and move *out*. Gradually, she found she had to give up parenting and let them go; to miss them without laying a guilt trip on them; to get back on her own, learn to think of herself again, and reclaim her independence. At times, it all seemed like a dirty trick!

THE PEOPLE IN YOUR LIFE

BEING GRANDPARENTS IN THE THIRD HALF

The life described above doesn't seem fair—until you discover the payoff that comes in the third half. When you get there, you'll find you have time to become good friends with your children, who will have children of their own. And they will understand *you* better and realize what a good job you actually did! You will be able to teach and play with your grandchildren. *And* you will have time for more quality experiences with your parents, who are moving into their later years. Life takes on a new kind of enjoyment.

Not What It Used to Be Either

Grandparenting is another arena in our lives that has been affected by the quiet revolution. For the silent generation, the change has been extraordinary. In their childhood, grandparents were an old couple wrapped in shawls, sitting in rocking chairs in front of the fire during a Sunday afternoon visit. Today grandparents go skiing together, have a game of softball, or go to the movies.

In her book *The Wonderful Crisis of Middle Age,* educator and family counselor Eda LeShan tells about watching *Strange Interlude,* the 1932 movie with Clark Gable and Norma Shearer. During the movie a couple ages, and by the end, "they look ready for the mortician—gray, wrinkled, palsied, tottering, quavery, barely able to walk." LeShan describes her shock when she realized that while they looked about a hundred, they were only in their sixties—*her* age. Well, the truth is that in those days, people expected to feel and look old. Age fifty-five meant nearing the end. Today, when we see two women and a child together, we can't be sure who is the mother and who is the grandmother.

There are more differences—ones that deal with child-raising. When people in the silent generation were children, their grandparents often lived with them, or at least nearby. Grandparents had status in the family—acting as counselors, advisors, and sharing in the responsibility for child-raising. Often they set the standards of discipline. This was an era when the two most common rules were "children are to be seen and not heard," and "if you spare the rod, you'll spoil the child."

Then when the silent generation became parents, Freud and Dr.

Spock appeared and child psychology took charge of child-raising. The result: the silent generation's parents were disenfranchised from the authority role that had been their model. It seemed that these new ideas would inevitably lead to less disciplined and spoiled children.

They didn't understand nor did they approve. They felt the loss of control, prestige and power. As a result, many of them backed off and the silent generation was left to find its way alone.

This is probably fortunate because the change in attitudes has been noteworthy and remarkable. Before the advent of child psychology, children were viewed as simply small adults and treated that way. Character was something to be instilled and developed by strict discipline and training. Children were vessels to be filled.

On the contrary, child psychology rightly teaches that children are born with a certain special individuality, an innate character that needs to be drawn out and developed, nourished, and encouraged. Most important of all, we have learned that, besides food and safety, a child's primary need is *real* love. This is not the mushy kind of love. Its characteristics are understanding, kindness, support, and caring. With enough of that kind of love, a child can make it—no matter what.

Giving Who We Are

Grandparenting today is a whole new ball game. We have a common understanding of children's basic needs. Henri Nouwen points out in his book *Life of the Beloved* that the most precious thing we have to give to another human being is who we are. This seems like a perfect role for grandparents. We can relax and enjoy our grandchildren, leaving the discipline, character building, and day-to-day worries to their parents. We can be ourselves with them, play with them, have fun together, share what we have that is uniquely us—and then send them home at the end of the day!

LeShan has a wonderful, inspiring approach: "What children need is someone who loves [them] crazily, blindly, and without reservation . . . [Grandparents ought to] let their grandchildren stay up later, eat more junk, bounce on the furniture, say dirty words, and get toys they don't need."

LeShan also adds that her daughter needs to understand that, just as she doesn't expect to tell her daughter what to do, when she's babysitting, her daughter can't tell *her* what to do either. "She isn't going to destroy my grandchild by her procedures, and I am not going to ruin her methods when I use my own once a week or once a month. Any kid in our family is going to be smart enough to know that mothers and grandmothers are not alike, and you have to learn to behave differently with each one . . . When he or she comes to visit we are going to have a ball. I'm going to regress. I'm going to bask in child's play. I'm going to make mud pies, or eat four hotdogs at the amusement park, and buy something ridiculously expensive at F.A.O. Schwarz . . . I'm not going to lecture on good study habits, or warn of the consequences of not drinking enough milk . . . That's Mama and Papa's job, not mine. I'm for laughs, for fun, for loving —nothing else."

"A Friend at Court"

There is another important contrast to "pre-revolutionary" ways. Because of the lack of understanding between the generations, people in the silent generation often protected their parents and children from each other. The children had to "behave" when grandma and grandpa came to visit and difficult things were never discussed. Today, that hopefully has changed to more open communications between parents and grandparents, more understanding because they are on relatively the same wavelength. LeShan also envisions a change in her relationship with her grandchildren. She dreams they will let her know their "imperfections, impulses, their less-than-lovely thoughts." She sees the grandparent role as that of "a friend at court."

A Second Chance

Grandparenthood is a wonderful, well-deserved second chance to enjoy little children who are special to us. Probably for most generations, being a parent has meant the same—spending a lot of time feeling too busy and tired, bewildered and lacking in understanding and experience; aware of the importance of this job, yet plagued by feelings of inadequacy. The wonderful news here is that there is a light at the end of the tunnel. A well-earned gift awaits you and that is grandparenthood!

One caution for those of you in the third half—you sometimes can get caught between your aging parents and your children, both needing time and support. It is possible to feel like the ham in the sandwich. Be careful to find a balance between taking care of yourself and taking care of your family. Don't let yourself become the ham that gets eaten up.

FRIENDSHIPS

As you make your transition from the second to the third half of life, friends become an essential ingredient that adds quality to your life. At any stage, friends bring understanding, closeness, and companionship. Now, as you shift roles, your whole social system will change more than you realize. Your business relationships are gone, so the old friends who stay close and the new friends you make will be attracted because of who you are—not what position you once held.

The third half gives you an opportunity to reach out to college chums and friends from your young-married years. Think of the people you have kept in touch with by exchanging Christmas cards. You may have written, "We really must see each other more often." But you never did, because of the pressures of career and family in the second half. Well, this is the time to do it. Chances are, you'll pick up right where you left off. And these old friends are usually some of your best friends.

This is also a great time to make new friends. You will be spending more time in the community, where there are a myriad of activities full of interesting, stimulating people. Getting to know them will enrich your life. The third half will be a time when gaps develop in the ranks of your regular friends—sometimes because friends are selling their family homes and moving to other communities; other gaps will occur because of death. To maintain a circle of friends, you must constantly make new ones.

Cultivating relationships is critically important now because you will be vulnerable to the loss of family and friends. You cannot count on one person or just a few to always be there for you. You also will be laying the foundation for your later years. There is convincing evidence that as the years go by, it is increasingly difficult to relate to people you have not known well or been close to before.

MEMBERSHIPS

In preparing for the third half, take a hard look at your memberships and affiliations. In the work life you are leaving, you may have gained satisfaction, stimulation, and a sense of belonging from your memberships in professional associations, business-oriented luncheon clubs, and men's or women's clubs. They may even have contributed to your career advancement, profit, or status. After all, *Who's Who* lists them, doesn't it?

But in these kinds of memberships, as in corporate life, when you're out, you're out. Trying to keep up these kinds of memberships after the race is over not only courts hurt feelings and resentments, it's expensive! Consider instead what memberships will produce the greatest satisfactions and feelings of belonging *in the future*. Perhaps it is church. Or yacht, tennis or golf clubs. Or reading groups, writing clubs, art societies—or whatever is your thing. Chances are, your community boasts Friends of the Library, Symphony Orchestra Auxiliary, Audubon Society, Retired Men's Association, Art League, Historical Society, and scores of similar groups that are eager to have new, active members. If you are planning to change to a new location (see chapter 12), the availability of meaningful memberships should also be a major factor in your decision.

COMMUNICATIONS—THE KEY TO GOOD RELATIONSHIPS

Good relationships with family or friends depend on good communications. We often think of communicating as speaking—making ourselves understood or getting a point across. However, especially in the third half, *listening* is just as important as speaking—probably even more so.

THE ART OF RECEPTIVE LISTENING

An expert in this field has said cynically but accurately, "The opposite of speaking is not listening; it is waiting—waiting, that is, for the chance to speak your own piece!" We are all too likely to do that. Good listening does not mean just keeping quiet and letting the other person talk. It means hearing not only the words the other person is saying, but the feelings expressed behind the words. Bottom line, the responsibility for good communication is not a fifty-fifty proposition. Because good listening is so important to the equation, the burden for good communication is largely on *you.*

When you listen well, you are showing respect for other people and for what they have to offer. Allowing them to express themselves freely, without interruption, enables them to feel their own individuality and worth. This kind of listening is so valuable and hard to find —people pay big prices to psychiatrists and therapists for it.

As you get older, good communication is a gift to the people around you—your spouse, children, grandchildren, and friends. How many times have you heard someone adoringly remember a grandparent who really listened to them and made them feel important! Your grown children may no longer welcome your efforts to parent them, but they usually appreciate a sympathetic ear when they need it.

We all have known people who, especially as they got older, became self-centered, interested primarily in their own health problems and operations, which they talked about endlessly. And they weren't interested in hearing about your concerns. Compare this to a chance encounter on a bus, plane, or at a social gathering when a total stranger gave you his or her complete attention (and vice versa) as you conversed? You were not giving or receiving advice or opinions; you were just *with* each other, offering a receptive, listening ear and warm responses. That is exactly the kind of communication *all* your relationships will benefit from.

VIVE LA DIFFÉRENCE

As you think about your relationships, it is helpful to realize that we are not all alike. Dr. Carl Jung grouped people into four types: those who *gather* data by sensation or intuition; and those who *process* data by thinking or feeling. Sensation types absorb specific facts. Intuition types take in general ideas and various possibilities. Thinking types reach conclusions by analysis and objective logic. Feeling types make quick judgements based on gut feelings. Jung also invented the familiar concept of extroverts and introverts.

How people function and communicate is based to some extent on their types. And how you relate to others can be facilitated by being aware of the various tendencies in these categories. (See the Bibliography for an easy to read book on this subject called *Please Understand Me.*)

Gender

Other and more familiar differences are those of gender. Better knowledge of these differences can improve relationships in marriage in the third half. Dr. Deborah Tannen, in her best-selling book *You Just Don't Understand,* says that women speak and hear a language of connection and intimacy, while men's conversation centers on a language of status and independence. She suggests that only by understanding these different styles can the two accept the differences and stop blaming each other.

Tannen traces this phenomenon back to childhood: "For girls, talk is a way *intimacy* is maintained. A little girl typically has a best friend, and they sit inside and tell each other secrets. When girls play in groups, they tend to make suggestions rather than give orders . . . Boys are likely to play in larger groups [and] . . . the groups have a hierarchy. The high-status boys give orders and push the low-status boys around. Talk is a way of negotiating status.

"As a result . . . men use language to get one-up on each other . . . it is defensive as much as aggressive."

When a wife wants something, she thinks that all she has to do is ask for it and her husband will do it. But his early warning system detects a sign he is being told what to do. To maintain his sense of independence, he puts off doing it. Genuinely puzzled and thinking she hasn't made herself clear, she repeats it and he hears this as nagging. Sound familiar?

Another of Tannen's insightful observations: "For a man, home is comfortable because it is a place where he is free to remain silent; for a woman, it is a place where she feels free to talk without being judged . . . For a woman, talk is the glue that holds a relationship together . . . Men feel that activities—doing things together—are what hold a relationship together. Talk is not central in intimacy for most men."

ACCEPTANCE—ANOTHER KEY TO GOOD RELATIONSHIPS

Above all, in any stage of life, realize and accept this fundamental fact: *you cannot change anyone else.* You can only change yourself. The more this kind of acceptance is a part of your way of life, the better your relationships will be.

Now, it is time to get out your pencil and notebook and ponder these important questions.

QUESTIONS TO EVALUATE YOUR RELATIONSHIPS:

- Are my relationships with friends and family what I want them to be? My spouse? My children? My grandchildren? How might I enrich these relationships?
- Do I have as many friends of both sexes as I want?
- Could I identify someone with whom I'd like to be friends and develop a meaningful relationship?
- Do I have some deep relationships—people with whom I can share my private thoughts and feelings? If not, would I like to? What might I do about it?
- Are my associations, my networks, working for me? Do I feel good about my group relationships and memberships?
- Are there things that need to be said between me and my significant other to help open up our relationship, give it more integrity, and make it more honest?
- Do I really listen to others and try to understand what they are feeling—as well as what they are saying?

9

From Work Life to
A Lifework Adventure

Whatever you can do, or dream you can . . . begin it. Boldness has genius, power and magic in it.
> *—Goethe, quoted by W.N. Murray*

Whatever happened to the passion we all had to improve ourselves, live up to our potential, leave a mark on the world? Our hottest arguments were always about how we could contribute. We did not care about the rewards. We were young and earnest . . .
> *—Wallace Stegner*

Risk

To laugh is to risk appearing a fool.
To weep is to risk appearing sentimental.
To reach out for another is to risk becoming involved.
To love is to risk not being loved in return.
To hope is to risk disappointment.
To try is to risk failure.
To live is to risk dying.

But risks must be taken,
Because the greatest hazard in life is to risk nothing.
The person who risks nothing—
Does nothing, has nothing, is nothing.

> That person has forfeited freedom.
> Only a person who risks is free.
> —Author Unknown

Your lifework—the work you choose in your third half—will be the culmination of all you have done in the past. Remember David Brown's words: "If you do nothing, you are already dead." Or, as one woman says, "After seven years of travel, bridge games and luncheon parties, I woke up and realized I was bored." In chapter 4, you saw that work is not only the natural condition of people, it can be absorbing, fulfilling, and exciting in the third half of life. It will also keep you in better physical, mental, and financial shape. In chapter 7, you discovered who you are. The next step is to begin planning, and this involves some further research.

TOM and BRENDA

Tom is pastor of a church in Connecticut. His wife, Brenda, also a minister, has been heavily involved in church-related work. They are planning for the third half of their lives. Ministers face a special situation, Brenda points out, in that they usually must move when they leave a church, thus forfeiting friends of many years as well as their identity with that community and their congregation. On the other hand, ministers always have a lifework. "What Tom and I are trying to do right now," she says, "is, in our thinking, to separate our present work life from our lifework."

An intriguing viewpoint! And a process that laymen must undertake as well. It is better to plan ahead for your lifework adventure from the vantage point of your second half work life. You can talk to people from your position of strength. You can control the timing of the change and manage it better.

Go back to the question of who you are. Have you some untapped potential as yet unused that could be your new avenue to fulfillment? Or have you had an experience that could lead into your own special lifework adventure?

· The story goes that Phyllis Diller once worked cleaning houses. She claims she used to go around envying others their looks, or their ability to sing, or whatever they could do well. Then after reading a book about believing in yourself, she got to thinking about what *she* could do that was special and recalled her reputation in high school for being funny. It was the beginning of her career as a successful comedian—and she is still going strong.

- A man suffered a nervous disorder late in his second half. He obtained effective help that turned his mental illness around. His experience made him aware when his son began to show the same symptoms, an indication this illness might be an inherited trait. He was able to intervene and get help for his son. Since then, he has retired from his second half career and entered his third half lifework in—you guessed it—the mental illness field for a smaller but sufficient salary. He is excited because he is doing important work to raise consciousness about the number of people with mental illness who *could* be helped, even though statistics show that only one out of five is being treated.

THE LIFEWORK ADVENTURE FORMULA

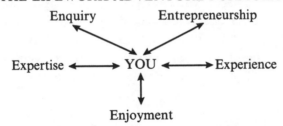

Enquiry   Entrepreneurship

Expertise ⟷ YOU ⟷ Experience

Enjoyment

We've already introduced three of the five "E" words that describe concepts essential to the lifework adventure formula. You have determined what you *Enjoy* doing—that is your values and interests—and where your *Expertise* lies. You have credited yourself with the fruits of your *Experience* and your accomplishments. To complete your formula, you need to *Enquire,* through research, what others need, and to bring an *Entrepreneurial* attitude to your third half. Let's take a closer look at the last two "E" words.

ENTREPRENEURSHIP

Freedom and flexibility characterize the third half of life for mature adults. Recognize this positive mind-set as your reality and you are ready for the best years of your life. And recognize that whatever lifestyle you choose involves risk.

There is risk not only in business but in any career or lifework choice. Doing nothing, doing nothing different, changing fields, learning new skills, changing locations, or lifestyle—all entail risk. It is your attitude toward risk that makes the difference. The spirit of the entrepreneur is in us all.

In this context, an entrepreneurial attitude toward one's lifework *may not* necessarily involve a business enterprise. It is more a matter of undertaking a project in a daring way that requires initiative. It does not mean financial or physical risk. Rather, we're talking about risking potential embarrassment if your plans should fall short of announced goals.

To be daring and adventuresome is fun—because we can be more like who we really are. We can expect some disappointment, failure, and discomfort—from which we can also expect to grow. Ours is a trial and error world. And as mature adults, we have the freedom to "go for it." The decision to embark on an "ad-venture" reflects a pioneering spirit, realistic optimism, and staying power.

ENQUIRY

You can enquire into possible lifework through two sources. The first is your public library, which contains reference books and periodicals, especially trade magazines. The second is *people*—your network of friends. It is said that by talking to just three people, there is hardly anyone you cannot reach. That is, you know someone who knows someone who can put you in touch with almost anyone you might want to meet. Thus your network can lead you to an expert willing to spend a half hour with you to give you information and help you sort out your options. (Be sure to keep research interviews separate from job interviews; if the subject of a job comes up, you should ask that it be deferred to another meeting for that purpose.)

FROM WORK LIFE TO A LIFEWORK ADVENTURE

A new phenomenon in the workplace is emerging just in time to be useful in your planning: so-called "contingent" work, or long-term temporaries. To achieve a more flexible work force and to reduce employee costs—particularly the overhead of employee benefits—companies increasingly are substituting "contingency" help for permanent employees. Such "temps" may be relatively long-term, not only in blue-collar jobs, but in managerial and professional positions. This trend increases the options open to you in the third half of your life. There is no age ceiling on temporary work.

BRANDT

Brandt left the Broadway theater after becoming "too old" (or so he felt) for male stage roles and later, for directing. Since he had some stenographic skills, he enrolled at a "temp" agency, which placed him to serve as secretary of the person in charge of travel, hotel, and convention services for a large professional association. *Within one week,* he was promoted to assistant, still on a temporary basis. When his boss left less than a year later, Brandt replaced him on the permanent payroll. He looks forward to going to work every day, including weekends. He is a favorite of association members, who say he is the best convention manager they've ever had.

You may also benefit from the decline in the quality of American education in a "knowledge" economy. Business is requiring more and more specialized technical and communications skills, which many recent graduates are not equipped to fill.

A public relations executive we know retired at sixty-five and decided that his values, interests, capabilities, and achievements all pointed to writing as a lifework in the third half. He started a "writing services" business, strongly doubting there was really a need for it. To his amazement and delight, clients have beaten a path to his door. He became so busy in his seventies that he had to bring in an associate. He feels his success is owed in part to the fact that many of "today's graduates of high school, and even of college, cannot write a coherent sentence. They are lacking to a shocking degree in vocabulary, spelling, punctuation, and grammar. So when people need something written clearly and fast, they turn to us who learned the basics back in the 1920s and 1930s."

Another beneficial aspect of the workplace of the 1990s is the fact that physical consolidation of "knowledge" workers is often no longer required. Computers, computer networks, modems, facsimile machines, cellular telephones—along with copiers and answering machines—offer such flexibility that you can work not only from your home but from your car, plane, train, or bus! No doubt further technological developments will make it even easier in the third half to carry on your lifework wherever and whenever it suits you.

As soon as your "people and paper" enquiries have identified some needs that might interest you, and which might utilize some of your capabilities, you're ready to evaluate how relevant your past accomplishments are. Lifework goals, projects, or missions will satisfy you most when they are congruent with your qualifications and background.

Whatever its source, once an idea is linked in your mind to the "market," it's time to become entrepreneurial. Assuming that the full-time career option has been replaced by the balanced lifestyle objective, lifework opportunities can be classified into three categories: civic involvement; consulting, teaching, and training; and small business.

CIVIC INVOLVEMENT

Civic involvement is an area that offers almost endless opportunities to do something that will "make a difference in the world." Many of the jobs are volunteer, but some offer compensation. Many involve only a few hours a week, others are full time. All can be rich in personal satisfaction and fulfillment.

From local animal shelters to symphony orchestras, there are countless organizations in need of people willing to dedicate their time, energy, and talents. To start you thinking in this direction, here's a sample of activities and places where you might find your niche:

· health care facilities—such as a hospital or nursing home;
· local institutions—the library, museum, or historical society;

- charitable or nonprofit groups—such as the American Red Cross, the YMCA/YWCA, the Boys/Girls Club, or the Association of Retarded Citizens;
- public and private agencies that support causes—such as the environment;
- adult education or tutoring;
- politics and government;
- mentoring "at-risk" school children

In response to Wallace Stegner's question, "Whatever happened to the passion we all had . . . to leave a mark on the world," we see limitless opportunities for most people in the third half. As the following examples show, all you have to do is supply the passion.

- A retired printing salesman with an affinity for books volunteers three days a week at his local library. The rest of the week he plays golf or spends time with his family. "I just can't wait for those days at the library," he confesses. "I help the schoolkids, I get to meet everybody in town, and the staff is so appreciative."
- A doctor in Florida, now retired over ten years from active practice, has made a commitment to keep up with his specialty and puts in a half day per week in a hospital emergency room.
- Immediately after her husband died, one woman in her sixties started part-time guided tours of an historic home. She also trains other widows to counsel recently widowed women in how to cope.
- A retired tax accountant has become a volunteer AARP tax aide, helping numerous older people with their returns.
- Following forty-three years with one company, a former sales administrator in New England converted his lifelong interest in politics into five years of service in his state legislature, being elected first to the House and then to the Senate.
- A former oil company executive has become deputy director of administration for one of the country's best-known museums.
- An ex-lobbyist, after a serious and unusual illness, became head of a national foundation sponsoring research on the illness.

If you yearn to leave your mark on the world, there are even institutions that will help you. For example, the University of North

Carolina at Asheville founded the N.C. Center for Creative Retirement. The center includes a non-credit College for Seniors, a Senior Academy for Intergenerational Learning, and a Seniors Leadership training course. While members of the center continue their own education, they often assist in the education of younger people, — both disadvantaged and undergraduates at the university. The Bush White House named the center one of the "Thousand Points of Light."

CONSULTING/TEACHING/TRAINING

Perhaps you lean toward consulting, teaching, or training. There are myriad opportunities in this category as well. Three volunteer organizations operating in this area cover your expenses only, but offer exciting lifework adventures:

- The International Executive Service Corps (IESC), referred to in chapter 5, matches the experience of retired executives with the needs of enterprises and government agencies in developing countries.
- A sister organization, the National Executive Service Corps (NESC), matches retired executives with non-profit organizations that have asked for help. The executives provide support to mainly educational, health care, social service, cultural, and religious institutions. For instance, a retired television executive has helped the local affiliate of a national health organization pull itself out of the doldrums by reorganizing its staff and board, and refocusing its fund-raising efforts.
- Volunteers in Technical Assistance (VITA) directly counsel the governments of developing countries. A former engineer and specialist in factory relocation who joined VITA after retirement has spent many months in China advising them on modernization.

Sometimes further education, which is itself enjoyable and absorbing, can lead to opportunities in a new field.

- A former chemical company lawyer with a latent interest in anthropology returned to university for an advanced degree in this science. He has since become associated with a leading anthropologist who is uncovering additional evidence of our link with prehuman existence.

· Bill Therivel, another former chemical engineer, became fascinated with the psychology of personality as it applies to self-development. This led to a Ph.D. for Bill, who observes:

> *"We can do marvelous things if we develop competence in a field in which we want to be active during retirement. The more competent we are, the more we can contribute, be appreciated and gain pride and satisfaction . . ."*
>
> *He says that having another interest in your second half of life contributes to a healthier attitude toward work. And it helps you prepare earlier for your later lifework.*
>
> *In the second half, ". . . we must perform for financial compensation and related rewards, building a family and finding ways to help our spouse and children be happy and grow . . ."*
> *In our third half, ". . . we perform according to different rules: We must be creative and help society—and have fun doing it— but without aiming for financial success.*
>
> *"The modern world badly needs competent and generous retirees to do all the things that cannot be delegated to [government] bureaucracies. Retired people can be the most modern, most efficient cure for many of the world's ills. All it takes is changing the way we look at things, the way we plan our lives."*

SMALL BUSINESS

Starting your own small business may appeal to you, as it has to many others. You may have an idea for a product or service that appears to meet a need. Go for it, bearing in mind certain precautions:

1. If your venture requires sizable capital, don't bet your family's grocery money!
2. Don't let your enthusiasm lead you to overcommit your time and energy. Even small retail businesses allow little or no time for leisure or family pursuits.

   One third-half couple we know were starry-eyed about opening a country inn. Within a year, they were tired of the daily cooking. She was sick of changing beds and he was crying for a little time off—a week maybe, or even a day!

3. One solution to both financial and personal demands is to take on partners or associates. But "living with" another personality in your third half may not be easy. Beware, the close association and mutual expectations can turn sour.

4. Be content to grow slowly. Expanding too fast or too soon can be disastrous.

5. Be sure your small business is satisfying in human terms, not just financially.

The nursery business described earlier is an excellent example of doing it right. Another example:

After twenty-five years as a buyer for a major clothing retailer, a woman lost her job as a result of downsizing. She was able to find a job in a small specialty house for less pay, but with "a piece of the action." She is now part owner.

Your business can take the form of a consulting or professional firm. These usually are a logical extension of your capabilities and experience. The writing services business mentioned before is an example.

Another businessman, good with his hands, began doing minor remodeling jobs for friends. He now successfully runs a small construction company.

Then there's the fanatic golfer who turned his hobby into a thriving business. He contracts with major tournaments, and with artists, to produce limited-edition prints of original paintings of the winners —signed by them.

A small business of your own—and, indeed, almost any lifework adventure you finally choose after your research—entails risk as well as reward. The risk is both financial and psychological.

Keep in mind, the entrepreneurial *attitude* is needed to engage in *any* new or unfamiliar action. Most people thrive on risks—because on the other hand, living just to be comfortable is boring. Challenges are creative and energizing.

Do what minister Ralph Ahlberg has exhorted his congregation to do: "I urge each one of you not to reach the end of your life without having championed some great cause, not without having confronted some impermissible outrage, totally, expensively if need be, energetically, with guts and nerve, with prayer and risk. That's how positive change happens."

There are numerous organizations that would welcome you. For a list of some of them, see "Information Resources" in the appendix. You may want to reread the quotes on risk featured at the beginning of this chapter, because they describe where you are right now. Isn't it time you took a risk—Go for it!

QUESTIONS TO DEFINE YOUR LIFEWORK ADVENTURE:

- How can I translate my personal experiences, interests, capabilities and values into a new project that will be interesting and exciting to me, as well as helpful to others? Can it include my spouse?
- Do I have a dream on the "back burner" of my life, some idea or project I have longed to spend some serious time on? Is there a "repressed crusade" that I have been itching to tackle all my life?
- What can be done about my dream or my crusade? What is there to learn? Where would I find teachers and people who can influence my results? Who is in my network?
- What would I *really* love to do in my third half? Would it afford the social contact, learning opportunities, and personal development I need?
- Will I want to work at home, or will I need a place that is separate from home? Will I want to work alone or with others?
- Do I really care? Do I have the discipline? Will it be fun? How much might it cost? How much might I earn?
- Can I quit working for pay? For the type of lifestyle I want, will there be a need for extra income? Am I being realistic? If I need some income, might I turn a lifetime hobby into a small business? Do I have the skills and experience to be an independent business person?
- How many hours a week, how many weeks a month, how many months a year do I want to work?

10

Your Financial Picture

The universal regard for money is the one hopeful fact in our civilization, the one sound spot in our social conscience. Money is the most important thing in the world. It represents health, strength, honor, generosity, and beauty as conspicuously and undeniably as the want of it represents illness, weakness, disgrace, meanness and ugliness. Not the least of its virtues is that it destroys base people as certainly as it fortifies and dignifies noble people.

—George Bernard Shaw

This is typical Shaw: outrageous, cynical, thought-provoking. Many would disagree with him, but his words do emphasize the importance of financial planning. Written by nonexperts, this chapter acknowledges that your financial picture must indeed be an intregal part of your life plan. The goal here is to *stimulate* your thinking.

IT'S A NEW DAY

Many people in their fifties and sixties have the house, car, and golf clubs or fishing boat paid for. Children are off the payroll. It's a new day!

But at first glance, the picture may not seem so bright. If you are just approaching the third half, your capital investments may be in the form of a yet-to-be "cashed" pension, a 401(k), an IRA, or other forms of savings. And even if all your children are through with college some may not yet be fully independent.

Nevertheless, financial security and your ability to maintain your current lifestyle when you enter your third half may be more in hand than you realize. Without a mortgage or other loans to pay off, without educational expenses for your children, and without full-time career clothing and transportation requirements, your cost of living will go down—to roughly forty percent to sixty percent of your current salary if you're in the middle income range. Some urban areas with high land costs may require more.

In doing forward financial planning for your future, there are two traps to watch out for. The first is scare tactics from financial advisors and other cassandras of the elderly political lobbies, who are likely to quote a requirement of eighty percent of your current salary. The second trap is your own inclination to spend excessively on special trips or other events, now that you are "saving" some full-time career expenses.

In any case, financial planning is essential to peace of mind. It needs to embrace all aspects: basic and discretionary expenses; dividend/interest/pension and business income; tax, estate, and investment planning; and health and life insurance. This is difficult. Most of us can barely deal with our income and expense budgets. Moreover, competent guidance on the other matters seldom resides in just one advisor, and it can be expensive.

What follows in this chapter is a general discussion and reminder of budgeting and planning issues. Part III provides a detailed outline, and guidance by a Wall Street expert, on making and managing your financial plans.

BUDGETING

One's personal financial statements include summaries of net worth, income, and expenses. If you are like most people who have bought real estate, you needed a mortgage. The bank required you to fill in a statement of your assets and liabilities (your current debts), noting the amounts and sources of your current income (with an assumption that it would be at least the same in future years), and your estimated expenses, including income taxes. Planning your finances for the third half requires that you repeat this process.

NET WORTH

Measuring net worth is like a snapshot in time of your investments (assets) less whatever you may owe to others (liabilities). To plan for the third half, you also need to look ahead to future years. Financial advisory firms have computer programs you can use—for a fee.

If you are like many people, your most significant income-producing assets will be your annuities. These will include your pension, your social security, and any other annuities you may have. A complete net worth statement should include a notation of the "present value" of these annual annuity receipts—in other words, a figure indicating the amount of capital that would be required to yield an equivalent amount of income from investments.

For example, if your investment portfolio is earning, say, ten percent before income taxes, your annuity income can be said to have a "present value" of ten times its annual amount. Some people fail to appreciate the value of these "savings" from their full-time careers. (This present value is a capital asset that you earned during your work life but could not, or did not, spend.)

If you are like many people, your most significant nonliquid asset is your primary residence. It is helpful to be realistic about its market value, which is typically used for your net worth statement. You can keep track of sales transactions of similar homes in your neighborhood, or you can pay a professional appraiser to do it for you.

What is important is to *know* what you are worth financially. That way, you can feel secure and have peace of mind, assuming that you keep the data current and continue to look realistically at the future.

INCOME

Tracking income is usually straightforward. Last year's income can come right off the first page of your federal income tax return. This year and the next—and five years out—are tougher, unless most of your income is "fixed," either in the form of annuities or bonds. The main concern (assuming your income is currently sufficient to pay your bills!) is to at least keep pace with inflation—to expect to be able to maintain your current purchasing power. Financial planning counselors have computer programs for this calculation, too—again, for a fee.

The sobering truth is that to have a healthy third half of life, your income must keep pace with inflation, if you want to maintain your standard of living and your quality of life. This concern raises investment planning issues discussed later in this chapter, and explained in greater detail in Part III. Needless to say, an *un*healthy life raises other issues such as health insurance.

EXPENSES

How you spend your money (and your time) reflects your values and interests. If you are hazy about your spending patterns, review all your checks and credit card charges for a calendar year. When you have summarized them into meaningful categories, separate them into two classifications: essential and discretionary.

Within the *essential* category, differentiate the basics—food, shelter, medical, clothing, transportation, and health insurance—from other family commitments and obligations. Family commitments would include educational expenses, life insurance premiums, principal and interest payments on loans, and income tax payments. Should there be insufficient income to cover these basics, then your third half will need to have a work-life component that provides continued income.

The first category of *discretionary* expenses includes expenditures for recreation and relaxation. This means travel, vacations, hobbies, clubs, entertainment, and "splurges"—which some people may feel are essentials. It is crucial to your financial peace of mind to understand how many of these expenses are required to sustain the quality of life associated with a full-time career. If your total income in the third half can be expected to be about half your current income (if you are in the middle income range), you ought to be able to sustain your current quality of life and have a little left over to add to savings and investments.

To recap, a certain portion of the discretionary recreation and relaxation budget can be identified as appropriate to maintain quality of life. The balance of income can be allocated differently from year to year among your other priorities, such as investments and charitable contributions. One third-half couple we know allocates about seventy percent of their annual expense budget for maintaining quality of life. For a typical year, this breaks down to about sixty percent essentials, twenty percent "fun," ten percent savings, and ten percent for contributions to worthy causes.

The provision for additional savings is noteworthy. If you have been in the habit of disciplined saving each year of your full-time career life, then a continuation of the habit is natural — and prudent in light of inflationary pressures.

Couples should review these matters together. If you are single, go over them with someone you trust. Expenses *can* be controlled — and even reduced — without seriously compromising your quality of life.

IF YOU ARE A WOMAN

Some women have a good understanding of financial matters. But, unfortunately, many have left investment planning, banking, income taxes, and finances to their husbands. Since women are likely to live five to seven years longer than men, if you are a woman preparing for the third half of your life, you would be wise to commit some time, brains, and energy to catching up with family finances.

If you are married, a few hours of getting "briefed" will do the trick, providing you keep yourself up to date. Also, you may want to take advantage of adult education classes.

A single woman really should have a personal financial advisor. If you have a significant investment portfolio, professional financial consultants can help. If your assets are modest, it may be more difficult to find capable help. One source of assistance may be an AARP volunteer in your area. They have a special program for this purpose.

You can also decide to educate yourself. A good place to start learning is Part III of this book. In addition to adult continuing education courses in your community, there are many books to read on this subject. You may also want to attend talks given by financial advisors hoping to attract new clients. Another resource: Long Island University in Southampton, New York, has established the National Center for Women in Retirement through a federal grant. Called PREP, the center offers video tapes and handbooks designed especially for women in the third half of life.

PLANNING ISSUES

The subject of finances raises a host of questions and issues that are the core of entire courses, curriculums, careers, businesses, and even industries. Here, briefly, are some important issues to consider to ensure your financial well-being both in the second half and third half of your life.

FINANCIAL PLANNERS AND COUNSELORS

Professional financial advice is not always cheap, or even necessarily right, for your particular situation. It is said, "Investigate before you invest." But how do you do that? After you've taken stock of your current financial position along with your plans for the third half, you can read and study and talk with people.

Usually for the third half, investors have three broad goals:

a) they want to establish dependable, regular income;

b) they want to maintain their purchasing power; and

c) they want an investment strategy that is long term.

To achieve these investment goals, you must communicate to your advisor both your life purpose(s), and your financial status. One point is clear: to assure mutual understanding of investment objectives an investor has to participate actively, at least to some extent.

Investment planning consultants charge in one of three ways, all of which offer distinct advantages and disadvantages:

- *Fee only* — no conflict of interest, but you may be at the mercy of "product" salesmen.
- *Fee and commission* — no conflict of interest, except on limited "products" offered.
- *Commission only* — no fee for advice, but they need you to buy and sell "products" on which they earn a commission.

Financial planning is claimed as a profession by any number of advisors and firms. So you should select a financial consultant with extreme care. Even though certification or registration is not rigorous, at least ask for professional credentials. One couple gave full discretionary power to a young person they became fond of; he cashed them out and disappeared. Just prior to the steep fall in crude oil prices in 1986, another couple accepted the advice of a highly recommended advisor to buy condominiums in Houston. There are any number of similar horror stories.

Choosing a financial planning advisor is challenging because there are only two criteria: *subjective*—how do you feel personally about the individual's integrity and judgement; and *objective*—what is the person's track record? The first can only be ascertained by your gut feelings about the person. The latter is usually not readily available quantitatively, only qualitatively by referrals.

DILEMMAS AND IMPONDERABLES

A number of dilemmas and imponderables cut across the full spectrum of financial planning and make decisions difficult. You at least need some understanding of how they might affect you, if you wish to participate in your financial/investment planning for the third half of life.

The dilemmas involve investment portfolio choices. For example, assume that Investor A owns a $200,000 home (mortgage free), has $25,000 per year of annuity income, and a $10,000 annual income from investments.

A's ASSETS:

Home	$200,000 (market value, no mortgage)
Investments	$100,000 (producing 10% pre-tax income)
Net Worth	$300,000
Annuity	$250,000 (based on 10 × pre-tax income)
Total Assets	$550,000

Although Investor A's net worth equals $300,000 plus $250,000 in annuities, A's investment portfolio of $100,000 amounts to less than one-fifth of total assets. Because the other assets are "locked up," A's choice of investment strategy is limited.

How might Investor A resolve some of the major dilemmas?

· *Income Appreciation versus Guaranteed Income*
  70% of A's income (the annuities) is "fixed" and pretty well "guaranteed," so any increase in total income must depend on investment strategy and results.

- *Capital Growth versus Safety of Principal*
  80%+ of A's capital is relatively safe, so a growth strategy for the portfolio emphasizing common stocks would be prudent.
- *Individual Securities versus Mutual Funds*
  Portfolio diversification in no-load mutual funds can target a 15–20% total rate of return on investments over the long term.
- *Inflation versus Purchasing Power*
  A 15–20% total return will increase A's annual income enough to cover 4–5% inflation of expenses per year.
- *Risk versus Reward*
  Any target total return on investments of less than 15% will be insufficient to sustain A's quality of life.

The strategy above is "aggressive," but *not* "speculative." It can be aggressive because so much of the income is dependable. If all the $35,000 income came from investments, the overall strategy could be more conservative, in effect fixing a portion of the income through, for example, government and corporate long-term bonds. However, some part of the overall strategy would still need to be aggressive.

Now for the imponderables. These are the external forces that impact businesses, stock and bond markets, and real estate markets. These forces include: government fiscal and monetary policies and practices, and regulatory practices; foreign trade and balance of payments; interest rates; and foreign currency relationships. Not even the most noted economists or government professionals understand fully how all these forces interact, especially now that there truly does exist a world economy. Trying to forecast political developments is virtually impossible, and is perhaps the fundamental reason why the third half is the time of life when most people expect to have conservative, long-term financial strategies.

If your investment strategy is truly long-term, then you do not need to worry about short term downturns in the economy or declines in stock or real estate markets. Your primary residence may be valued at $200,000 currently, jump up to $225,000 next year, and fall to $150,000 the following year. But if you're not planning to sell and relocate soon, so what? Your $100,000 mutual fund investment may gyrate wildly at times, too. Unless you are intending to cash out though, it's just figures on paper. What is real is the dividend flow, and chances are you will see very little change from one year to the next. What you want is steady growth that helps you keep pace with, or even pass inflation rates.

INVESTMENTS

With new technologies and fast-changing markets, the number and type of financial products and services available has become increasingly complex. For peace of mind, be sure you understand and are comfortable with what you have.

Most financial planning guides use four investment categories: defensive, conservative, aggressive, and speculative. Using the example of Investor A, the fixed income annuities (for example, pension and social security payments) are "defensive"; the personal home is considered "conservative"; and the mutual fund is "aggressive."

Defensive investments connote no growth, either in principle or income, because they're oriented to perform well in conditions of zero inflation or deflation. This would be typical of most pension arrangements but not U.S. Social Security payments, which are adjusted in line with the consumer price index in order to offset inflation.

Conservative investments connote "balanced" growth, that is, income that barely keeps pace with inflation, after taxes. In A's situation, residential real estate values historically have averaged growth in line with the economy over the long term.

Aggressive investments connote income and principal growth somewhat in excess of the rate of inflation. As illustrated previously, successful investments in this category can offset the "drag" of defensive investments, and keep your overall situation on an even keel in spite of inflationary trends.

Some investors have more flexibility than Investor A. If so, an asset allocation strategy would still be required. We can use Investor A's situation to illustrate this point.

Suppose A was renting his or her primary residence and all of A's capital was represented in an investment portfolio of $550,000 (all of A's assets). Investor A would be well-advised to spread this $550,000 of capital assets over the same three categories, that is, defensive, conservative, and aggressive, perhaps in even proportions. On the other hand, if A really expects four percent to five percent inflation indefinitely, the defensive category could be reduced. Clear communication of A's third half of life purpose will provide the key element in determining of A's asset allocation strategy.

INSURANCE ISSUES

Some personal insurance coverage is a "given," for example, health and medical insurance, and property and casualty insurance for your house and car. About the only "issue" around such coverage is how big a deductible or coinsurance feature to have in order to reduce premiums and still obtain appropriate protection.

Two serious issues related to health and medical insurance concern (a) long-term care services, and (b) major medical coverage for children who are still dependent. Planning for long term care is difficult for many people: they can plan to stay at home or live with relatives; they can buy long-term care nursing home insurance with annual premiums; or they can invest in a life-care residential facility with monthly maintenance. Too many people fail to address this issue far enough ahead. You owe it to yourselves, your children, loved ones, and friends to do so.

Many people have, or will have, children whose initial career income is insufficient to pay for personal medical insurance. Apart from insisting that should be a high priority, you need to arrange protection for them in the short term. When a child is not covered, an unforseen catastrophic accident or illness can wipe out parents— not by law, but by love.

Another significant insurance issue concerns personal liability coverage. In our litigious society, many advisors urge the purchase of this type of protection. It typically can be obtained only from the company that carries both your homeowner and automobile policies. If your net worth is substantially more than the standard personal liability provisions in your home and car coverage, "excess" personal liability insurance is probably prudent, and it is relatively inexpensive.

Life insurance presents an additional set of issues. This is because of the range of options—from what is really pure *death* insurance (called "term" insurance) to various combinations involving death insurance coupled with an investment feature ("whole life," "endowment," or "single premium"). A word of advice for those of you who have worked for an organization that offers a life insurance fringe benefit: If you are able to retain it after you leave at a low-cost premium available through group rates, this is usually advisable. Coverage beyond that is very personal, and should be coordinated with your investment and estate strategies.

If you are going to be eligible for a pension that you will take as an annuity, in most cases, you will have several options. The highest monthly amount will be payable only to you in your lifetime. If you prefer, reduced monthly payments will be available, for example, for "ten-years certain," or to provide for your spouse in the event you predecease him or her. Before you make your selection, evaluate the possibility of using "term" insurance in combination with the highest annuity payment option; it may be that the premium will be less than the amount of the reduction in your particular plan. In addition, the insurance has estate planning advantages associated with passing on assets to your heirs.

ESTATE PLANNING

Decisions regarding investment strategy, income taxes, insurance, and your year-to-year budgets have a direct bearing on your estate planning. For a complete outline of estate planning issues, see chapter 17.

It is difficult to carry out prudent estate planning without a lawyer who specializes in this field. Of all the professional services you'll need in order to manage your finances well, the most critical one is a lawyer. In some ways, you'll need an attorney who understands you and your family as well as, or even better than, you understand yourself. What are your values, what are your lifework goals, what is the meaning and purpose in your life?

Remember, there are two kinds of "trust" you must have in your advisors. The first is the obvious one of honesty and ethics. But you must also trust their judgement to be consistent with your lifestyle, financial, and personal objectives.

QUESTIONS TO FOCUS YOUR FINANCIAL PICTURE:

- Are all your records in order, where you can find them, and where your family members can find them?
- Is your expense budget clear and workable?
- Do you have a good fix on expected after-tax income for the next few years?
- Have you calculated your net worth? Is it clear how much is liquid and how much is not? Is your debt level where you want it?
- Are you comfortable with your advisors—lawyer, insurance agent, tax accountant, financial consultant?
- Have you gone over these issues with your family? It is a good idea.

11

Learning and Leisure

Ideally, the third half of your life should be a three-way balance of new lifework, ongoing learning, and newfound leisure. Thus far we have concentrated on the work part of the equation. Let's take a look now at learning and leisure.

LEARNING

Learning can be a lifelong delight. You may look back on your high school and college experiences as exciting and enjoyable (many do!). Or you may remember them as an ordeal. The silent generation grew up in an era when education was synonymous with being taught, with having information drilled into them. But true learning has been described as letting the seed of knowledge blossom within you. In any case, ongoing learning is especially important in your third half for a number of reasons:

1. It is a constant source of pleasure for its own sake.
2. It opens new windows, preventing your life from becoming too closed to new ideas and too self-oriented as you age.
3. It makes *you* more interesting.
4. It may lead you to whole new avenues of worthwhile endeavor.
5. It helps keep your mind alert and active.

In your second half of life, reading for pleasure or general edification was probably a rare luxury to be squeezed between the demands of a career and a growing family. But in the third half you can set aside as much time as you like for reading, attending lectures, or even taking courses you somehow missed.

BOB

Bob, the man in an earlier chapter who started a "writing services" business at age seventy, says that, in addition to its keeping him extremely busy and productive, "the greatest bonus is that I am always *learning*. I usually have to do research on the books or magazine articles I am hired to write. One day it is mountain lions in the Rockies; the next it is mental retardation or the history of our town in Revolutionary days. I may be writing a book on nutrition along with a magazine article on new ways to aid farmers in third world countries. I'm always interviewing fascinating people who make things happen.

"I tend to become personally involved with whatever I'm writing about. My wife says I'll burst into the house at the end of a day, saying things like, 'Guess how many descendants a mother housefly could produce in a single April-to-September season, if they all survived.' (The answer, incidentally, is 336 trillion, in nine generations.)

Now I'll grant you, it's kind of hard to work that into a cocktail-party conversation, but I *do* know a lot more about more interesting subjects than I used to, which I thoroughly enjoy. I am constantly learning."

Liz Carpenter, retired secretary to Lady Bird Johnson, wrote about her philosophy of learning in *Greenwich Magazine*. She was eighty-five at the time:

> *Renewal is the idea that my friend, John Gardner, seventy-two, founder of Common Cause, returns to again and again. He states it so appealingly that I find myself asking each day, "What can I do to renew myself?" There's a myth that learning is for young people. But as the proverb says, "It's what you learn after you know it all that counts." Learn from your failures. Learn from your successes. When you hit a spell of trouble, ask "What is this trying to teach me?"*

People learn from their jobs. They learn from their friends and families. They learn by accepting the commitments of life, by playing the roles that life hands them, by getting older, by suffering, by taking risks, by loving and bearing life's indignities with dignity.

The lessons learned in maturity aren't simple; they go beyond the acquisition of information and skills. You learn to avoid self-destructive behavior. You learn not to burn up energy in anxiety. You learn to manage tension. You learn that self-pity and resentment are among the most toxic of drugs. You learn to bear the things you can't change. You learn that most people are neither for you nor against you; they are thinking about themselves. You learn that no matter what you do, some people aren't going to love you.

As a rule, you have to put some miles behind you and some dents in your fenders before you understand those things. As Norman Douglas has said, "There are some things you can't learn from others. You have to pass through the fire."

To keep your zest until the day you die, I offer a simple maxim: "Be interested." Everyone wants to be interesting, but the vitalizing thing is to be interested. Age must not trap you in a one-dimensional world. Keep a sense of curiosity. Discover new things. Care. Risk failure. Reach out.

Carpenter goes on to tell how, after her family's departure, she knocked down some walls in her home to put in a hot tub that seats "eight friends or six enemies" plus a room with a massage table. "Friends like to come for the evening to enjoy a soak and a rubdown by a masseuse who makes house calls . . . Rather than be buried or cremated, I would like to be bronzed sitting in my Jacuzzi, spouting hot water." She ends her article with some favorite free verse by an Englishwoman named Jenny Joseph:

When I am an old woman, I shall wear purple
With a red hat which doesn't go, and doesn't suit me.
And I shall spend my pension on brandy and summer gloves
And satin sandals and say we've no money for butter.

I shall sit down on the pavement when I'm tired
And gobble up samples in shops and press alarm bells

And run my stick along the public railings
And make up for the sobriety of my youth.

I shall go out in my slippers in the rain
And pick the flowers in other people's gardens
And learn to spit . . .

But maybe I ought to practice a little now
So people who know me are not too shocked and surprised
When suddenly I am old and start to wear purple.

WRITING

Carpenter's article illustrates how fun writing can be in the third half of life. Personal writing is something anyone can do. Keep a diary or journal. Write memoirs to share with your children and grandchildren, who will marvel at what the world was like when you were their age. Write letters to friends and relatives—or even "letters to the editor." Letter writing is virtually a lost art in this age of media and entertainment overload. But it can be a stimulating learning experience.

Get Some Equipment!

By all means buy a computer, a printer and a fax machine—and learn how to use them. Nothing will bring you more quickly into today's world, and you'll be making a definite statement about your attitudes and openness to new ideas. Besides, it's great fun! You don't need to know how or why they work; just enjoy their fabulous capabilities.

The proprietor of the "writing services" business quoted earlier admits he was stubbornly resistant to any improvement in writing machines since his pre–World War I manual typewriter that he had used for a half century. But when he started his business at age seventy, he reluctantly recognized he *had* to use a computer. "I learned everything I needed to know in order to use WordPerfect software for writing in about two hours. A piece of cake! And what an improvement!"

LEISURE

Leisure should become a high priority as you plan the third half of your life. Just keep in mind that the traditional concept of retiring to a life of a hundred percent leisure is a snare and a delusion.

GERRY

Gerry was a man who, in his second half of life, always looked forward to his weekend golf. As his retirement approached, and people began to ask what he planned to do, he would reply, "I'm going to play golf every single day. I can hardly wait!" And he did, for about eighteen months. During that time, he found that old golfing buddies from his company and business associations gradually drifted away. To make up for it, he hooked up with a group of retirees at his club who played twice a week. "They were awfully inbred," Gerry complains. "They sniped at each other going around the course, and back at the clubhouse, they bickered over the score. After a few weeks, I said to myself, 'This isn't much fun.' "

He persisted, however, in playing almost daily for a year and a half. "Then one day, as I was getting out of bed for an early tee-off time, it dawned on me that this was like commuting to work." Gerry's love of the game did not diminish, but from then on, he scheduled his golf as a leisure pursuit—and not the main objective of his life.

Now is your opportunity to set aside time to do what you especially enjoy: tennis, fishing, hiking, camping, boating, gardening, reading, building ship models, painting, listening to good music—whatever your list includes. You may even want to try a sport or activity you've never done before.

One man from the south took up skiing after he retired at age sixty. By sixty-five, he could (and did!) drop the names of fashionable ski resorts in the Alps, where he became a ski bum every winter, with the blessing of his wife who went off to enjoy her favorite spa. He loved not only the skiing, but the opportunity to meet new and interesting people of all ages.

TRAVEL FOR LEARNING AND FOR LEISURE

Ask most people what they plan to do in "retirement," and they'll answer "travel." Travel can be the ultimate learning or leisure experience — *with proper planning and proper balance in your third half of life scheme.*

Travel for its own sake quickly palls. But travel for the purpose of learning is particularly rewarding. Many universities, college alumni associations, museums, and magazines such as *Smithsonian, Audubon, Natural History, Sierra, Military History, Civil War Times* sponsor tours. So do professional tour organizations. Your pleasure on such trips will be enhanced if you study the local history and culture in advance.

One newly retired couple leased a motor home and began a planned itinerary around the whole country. Upon their return nearly twelve months later, the wife said, misty-eyed, "It was just the most wonderful, worthwhile year of our life. I can't describe to you the warm feelings and emotions of seeing some of our best friends we had all but forgotten. With our own accommodations in the motor home, we felt we were never intruding — though many times our hosts simply *insisted* we stay with them! I know that because of this new circle of dear people, the rest of our life will be better."

Other couples we know have accomplished the same thing by driving their own cars and staying in inexpensive motels, or by a combination of flying and renting cars at select destinations. The important thing is to see old friends once again — which is one of the most heart-warming reasons to travel.

There is an almost endless variety of special interest groups that sponsor tours for golfers, tennis players, art and architecture enthusiasts, and so on. If you are a member of Alcoholics Anonymous, Al-Anon or similar self-help groups, there are over three hundred conferences and conventions per year in the United States and Canada for you to attend. Likewise, travel agencies put together "Sober Sailors" cruises and group trips to Hawaii, Alaska, Europe and elsewhere — with meetings held en route!

BEATING THE AGE GAME

THE LEAST EXPENSIVE ROUTE

If money is a problem—and travel *can* be expensive—try the fine tours offered through the AARP or Elderhostel programs. You may stay in university dormitories or share a bath, but the accommodations are comfortable and the cost is modest. Here are more tips from seasoned budget travelers:

- Plan your own trip, rather than going through a travel agent.
- Go during off-season periods when airfare and lodging are often reduced.
- If you plan a long stay, rent a house or apartment instead of staying in a hotel or inn.
- For even longer stays, rather than renting a car, buy a used one through a dealer that offers buy-back agreements.
- Stay in lodgings and eat at restaurants frequented by locals.
- Stay at bed-and-breakfast inns or tourist homes—which are perfectly reputable, but offer fewer amenities.
- If you are visiting well-known tourist attractions, the farther away you stay, the less expensive it will be. Chains such as Motel 6 or Super 8 cater to seniors at a fraction of the cost of a Disneyland Hotel or a Yellowstone Lodge.

If you don't hunger to travel now, just browse along the travel shelves of your local bookstore. The full-color cocktail-table type books and the guidebooks will surely whet your appetite.

Now, get your notebook and begin making your learning and leisure plans.

QUESTIONS TO IDENTIFY YOUR LEARNING, LEISURE, AND TRAVEL INTERESTS:

- What would I like to learn:
  Painting? Another language? Computer? Singing? Gardening? Financial investing? Cooking? Literature? Writing? Bridge? Piano? Guitar? What else?
- Where would I love to travel to and explore:
  More of the good old USA? The culture of Europe? The exotic East? Africa? By boat, rail, plane, bike, hiking, skiing?

· What am I going to read:
  Biographies? Novels? History? Do I want to take courses or join
  a reading group?
· Which of the arts would I like to get into:
  Music? Painting? Sculpting? Crafts? By visiting museums or attending concerts? Theatre? Ballet?
· How am I going to get my daily exercise:
  Swimming? Fast-walking? Rowing? Biking? Gardening?

Everyone will have a unique list. In fact, making the list and beginning to visualize its contents in your new life is almost as much fun as doing whatever it is. Do both!

Where to Live

Take it slow, take it slow
You don't ever have to go.
Because it's blue skies here
From now on.
                    —Johnny Mercer

Few major decisions in life are made as impulsively as the one to move somewhere else after retirement. Hey, folks, it's not mandatory! But before the ink is dry on the pension papers, many couples pull up stakes and head for Florida, Arizona, or another Sunbelt destination.

Even for the less impulsive, the question of whether to stay put remains uppermost in their minds. That's where it *should* be. Like most other preparations for the third half of life, the decision of where to live deserves careful thought and planning. Above all, "Take it slow, take it slow. You don't ever have to go."

Let's look at how five couples handled this decision:

ROGER and CYNTHIA

Roger, a skilled carpenter, owned a small construction company. Cynthia had worked for fifteen years in the admissions office of a local community college, helping to finance their three children's educations and contributing to their retirement nest egg. Approaching the third half of life, they had lived in the same home for thirty-five years and had two of their grown children nearby plus two grandchildren, who meant a lot to them both.

Neither of them had thought much about retirement, although Roger, who often had to work outside in the cold and wet of winter, warmed himself with dreams of living in a sunny clime. Cynthia confesses that her only thought of retirement was that she might be able to sleep late! Then, one winter day, a younger man came along and offered Roger a good price to buy his business. He enthusiastically reported the offer to Cynthia, adding his fantasy of moving south and "taking it easy." He would buy a boat and spend his time fishing, he said. Without giving it much thought, Cynthia agreed. It would be nice to be warm and they would make a new life. She left her job at the college, and they moved to Florida.

Suddenly Cynthia found herself in a strange place without family or friends. When Roger was out fishing, she began to feel frightened and alone. She missed her children terribly, especially the grandchildren. There were no youngsters in their new community. All the people seemed old to her. She longed to be with her many friends back at the college. For his part, Roger enjoyed his boat and his fishing, but soon began to feel bored and vaguely restless.

After only a few months, they talked it over and decided they had jumped too quickly, with too little thought. The problem was, having sold their house, moving back would be expensive. However, they decided that their future happiness was worth it, so they returned.

LUCY and JOHN

John was an accountant with a large company in Texas. While he devoted thirty years to his career, which he loved, Lucy managed their home, raised their children, and took an active part in civic organizations.

When they began to look ahead to the third half, two of their sons had located in Maine. John was beginning to tire of his routine, so they considered moving to Maine. However, it was a long way from home and the many friends they had made over a lifetime. Also, the culture and climate were very different. Because it would be such a major move, they agreed to experiment before making their final decision.

They began taking their vacations in Maine, renting a house in the same town as their sons, and their families, usually staying a month or two to see if they liked it. Lo and behold, they loved it! Each time they went back, they felt more and more at home. They enrolled in our life planning seminar, where they were able to stand back and ask themselves the hard questions: Would we be leaning too much on our sons up there? How would we get involved in some lifework so far from our roots and contacts? Which, if any, of our values, capabilities, and interests would fit in Maine and which would be lacking? Above all, what would everyday life year-round be like in Maine?

Finally, their decision was almost made *for* them. One of their sons asked John to join him in his little entrepreneurial company as financial officer. Meanwhile, Lucy had become active in a local environmental organization. Five years had elapsed from the first time they thought of moving to Maine; now they were *sure* it was the right decision.

Lucy and John have never looked back. Although they missed their old friends, just as they had anticipated, they took care of that with visits. They developed new friends. And their choice has been a happy one.

GEORGE and GINGER

George and Ginger had lived in a large, sumptuous home on the water, within commuting distance of New York City, where George was a CEO. They were constantly surrounded by the families of their four grown children, which they reveled in, and led an active social life.

When George retired without a specific plan, they sold their house for a good price during the real estate boom of the 1980s. George decided abruptly that they should simplify their lives (not a bad idea in itself!), get away from the expensive town in which they lived, and reduce their extravagant lifestyle. Their solution was to move to a roomy, pleasant condominium in a retirement community about forty miles away. (They did, however, retain second summer and winter homes.)

Their children, who had grown up in the original town, were not particularly eager to visit the condominium. In fact, visits of grandchildren were severely limited by covenants in the "adult community," and were frowned on by the neighbors. George's and Ginger's old friends were glad to come for dinner a time or two, but the long drive slowly discouraged frequent socializing.

Since the retirement community was built around a golf course, Ginger had envisioned George playing every day. But as it turned out, he didn't have much interest in the game. They hadn't met any fellow residents before buying their condo, and it turned out they had little in common with them. "We are fish out of water," complained George.

Then it turned out that the developer had retained ownership of the golf course, and he proposed to close it and use the land for more condominiums. The owners' association was up in arms, naturally, and took the matter to court—so George found himself assessed for the legal expenses to fight for a golf course he wasn't interested in anyway. To make matters worse, the community sewage plant, which the developer *had* turned over to the association, was inadequate for the growth that had taken place. So it had to be rebuilt, which meant another legal suit. More costs. More assessments. More aggravation.

"Okay," says George, "I admit we made a big mistake. We'd like to move back—to a more modest place this time. But with the recession and the bottom dropping out of real estate, it's almost impossible to sell anything in our new community. There are the 'adults only' restrictions plus all the headaches and legal problems. Believe me, we don't need this kind of mess at our age."

MIKE and MARY ALICE

Mike and Mary Alice had spent their entire lives in a small Oklahoma town, where Mike had been a successful oil man. They had two grown sons who were also well off. With admirable zest for living and the means to afford the best, they were great travelers in this country and abroad.

An earlier illness had left Mike with severely impaired eyesight, so for decades, Mary Alice had the task of driving her husband, whether on business or pleasure. Western Oklahoma is barren land with long cheerless winters, so as they approached their third half of life, they rented a small house in a retirement community in Arizona for the winter months.

This town is a well-planned community with many golf courses, each with club facilities. There are a number of handy shopping centers, health clubs, and huge swimming pools. Mike and Mary Alice took to their new surroundings immediately. They found a much more diverse population than at home, with people who were easy to meet. The clincher, however, was that Mike could drive to the club, the pool or the grocery store in an electric golf cart which he kept in his garage—as did many of his neighbors. For the first time since either of them could remember, Mike was independent and Mary Alice was relieved of her chauffeuring chores!

After several winters there, Mike and Mary Alice gave up their Oklahoma house and moved to Arizona permanently. In the hot summer months, they rent a condominium in Utah, nestled in the mountains. They planned carefully, tried out their new spot before they moved, and now they are completely happy with their decision.

BOB and BEVERLY

Bob and Beverly compromised: They live in two places at once. Bob was a respected cardiologist in Little Rock, Arkansas. His wife, Beverly, was a capable homemaker, hostess, and mother to two grown daughters. In his late fifties, Bob suffered a severe heart attack himself. He says, only partly jokingly, "My heart patients tended to have less confidence in me after that, so I retired."

They had skied several times in Idaho, where they admired the spectacular mountain scenery and were enchanted with the healthy, relaxed, yet sophisticated lifestyle. So in Bob's forced retirement from practice, they rented a condominium for the winter to see how they liked it. The ski season was as invigorating and enjoyable as they remembered. They then rented in the summer, when Arkansas is hot and humid. Bob plunged into the fabulous fishing and Beverly said, "The Idaho summer weather, dry and sunny during the day and so cool at night you need a blanket, is just an undiscovered bit of heaven."

So they purchased a sizeable, comfortable house in a rural area of Idaho. However, they still loved Little Rock, where they had family, warm friends, and deep roots. Says Beverly, "We love the azaleas and magnolias in the Arkansas spring, and Bob would miss his bird hunting in the fall. So we just live in two places now: in Little Rock in the spring and fall; and Idaho in the winter and summer. We think we have the best of both worlds!"

Bob adds, "We've met a number of couples our age in Idaho who follow the same pattern. And as it worked out, we see a lot of our children and grandchildren, and our Arkansas friends as well, in Idaho. The house is seldom empty!"

MOST STAY WHERE THEY ARE

The previous stories represent a minority. Surveys show that ninety percent of Americans in the third half of life live within ten miles of where they have always lived. They may move to a smaller house or to a different part of town, but most people decide to stay rather than move. Here are some considerations to help you pinpoint your ideal location.

· Your *personality type.* Are you introverted or gregarious? The later in life you move, the harder it is to make new friends. But it's easier if you're gregarious.
· Your *state of health.* How close to a doctor or a hospital do you want to be? Moving introduces new stresses that you may not want to face.
· Are you a *nester or a vagabond?* "Our house is a very important

emotional anchor for me," says one woman. "It gives me support and identity—and maybe even status, if I admit it. So even if we travel a lot or have a second home which we love, I don't want to give up my house. I would feel like I'm drifting." Her husband, on the other hand, says he's tired of maintaining the "big house" and the lawn. He hears the call of the open road, and would like nothing better than to sell the house, buy a trailer, and see the country.

· Your *financial situation.* If you are tempted to move for a better tax break or lower living costs, be careful. Countless retirees move to Florida not only for the warm climate but because it has no inheritance tax and housing is cheap. But parts of Florida have grave problems—lack of water, a damaged environment, crime, inadequate schools, and simply too many people. One newly arrived couple on a modest, fixed income recently complained, "Sure, the house was inexpensive, but we hadn't figured on having to water the lawn year-round, and the water rates are astronomical. We don't have heating bills, but that's more than offset by the cost of air conditioning year-round."

· The *climate.* Many retirees have a passionate desire to "get away from the white stuff." But one couple we know says, "When the hard frost comes, we head *north.* We love winter, with the crunch of snow underfoot and frosty breaths, brisk walks and winter sports, and sitting around a blazing fire at night." (Maybe they have discovered, like so many people, that the secret to staying warm is the new silk underwear from L.L. Bean.)

In any case, like four of the five couples in the stories above, if you are considering moving in the third half, it is advisable to rent first for at least a few months, and preferably a year or two. Living someplace as a resident is different from vacationing there. It will give you time to make sure that: (1) you fit, (2) you like the people and they like you, (3) you know the disadvantages and advantages of the new location. Like getting married, it's better to know ahead of time—because changing your mind is difficult and expensive.

TAKE IT SLOW!

While most retired couples with children gone want to move into a smaller place, don't hurry into a space that may prove *too* small. You may need more work space than you think for your projects and activities; and you may need flexibility for visiting family and friends.

If you are considering moving to a "retirement" community while in your fifties and sixties, take it very slow indeed. Make sure the environment is compatible with your chosen lifework and leisure interests. Beverly, featured in an earlier story, says they find being surrounded by active, attractive, younger people is stimulating and helps keep them young. Another lady declares flatly, "If I had to, I'd rather live in an apartment over somebody's garage than move to the best retirement community."

LIFE-CARE COMMUNITIES

Of course, as you require more care in your later years, a life-care facility can be a perfect solution and your most viable choice. If and when that time comes, facilities that offer several stages and a full range of care are preferable. Examples include independent living through assisted care, custodial care, physical rehabilitation, intermediate nursing, full nursing, and mental care. Purchase prices and maintenance fees for life-care facilities vary according to location, the range of services provided, and the quality and spirit of management and staff.

BETH

When she turned eighty-five, Beth, a widow from Rhode Island, opted for a life-care place where a friend was living. She purchased a beautiful apartment with a nice terrace and garden that looked out on a lake. Although she had made many good friends where she lived before, she had begun to feel lonely and lacked the energy to entertain.

At the life-care community, Beth found a built-in social life. She welcomed the chance to go to a dining room for dinner every night. And, although not interested in marrying again, she enjoyed the camaraderie with men, as well as women, with whom she played golf and enjoyed swapping jokes and stories.

Beth made many good friends, became part of the place, and liked living there immensely. She wrote articles for the "village" newspaper, created flower arrangements (which she had always loved to do) for the central living room, and became an "institution" in the place until well into her nineties.

Then, needing more assistance, she moved into the "dependent care" facility where staff was readily available, yet her friends were welcome to visit her. She felt at home, living there happily until age ninety-eight, when she died.

Retirement communities can be a wonderful solution to old age. Beth's experience was born out in *The Wall Street Journal,* in a recent article about a study of centenarians in Georgia. The scientists expected to find these people depressed, melancholy, and frail; instead, they found humor and optimism among people who were busy fishing and riding bikes.

The bottom line is that "where to live" is not the be-all and end-all issue of your third half. You can only change so much by changing the scene around you. Wherever you go, you take yourself with you! "Take it slow . . . You don't ever have to go . . . It's blue skies here from now on."

As you think about your situation and where you want to live, get out your notebook and pencil and go through the following questions about your "ideal place."

QUESTIONS TO DETERMINE WHERE
YOU'D LIKE TO LIVE:

- What work life and learning opportunities would there be?
- What population characteristics do I want?—Large? Small? Homogeneous? Heterogeneous?
- Where or what would it be near—a big city? University? Lake? Mountains? The sea?
- What do I want the social and cultural environment to be like?
- What religious and spiritual opportunities are available? Do I fit in? How will I take care of that part of my life?

- What kind of climate would I like?
- What sports and recreational facilities do I want—a golf course? Tennis courts? Walking trails? Fishing streams?
- Are there good healthcare facilities and services available? Do I need some special ones?
- What about transportation, locally and for traveling? Is there an airport or bus station?
- What sort of housing environment do I want?—Condo? Home? Neighbors? Do I want to be close to my family? Or an hour or two away?
- What cost of living can I afford? (See chapter 15)

13

Health and Wellness

If I knew I was going to live this long, I'd have taken better care of myself.

> —*Jazz pianist and composer Eubie Blake, on turning 100*

There's a lot of wisdom in Eubie's comment. For what counts is not the length of life but the quality of life. And your health is a crucial factor in the quality of the third half of your life. The good news is that the kind of health you will enjoy as you grow older is largely up to you. You can take charge of your life *now* and make changes that will influence your health in later years.

THE CHICKEN OR THE EGG QUESTION

Are people active because they are healthy, or are they healthy because they are active?

MARIE

Marie was a young woman with exceptionally good health. In midlife, she was still walking daily and playing tennis regularly. But as she approached the third half, she became lazy and sedentary. She ate more, especially snacks, and allowed herself to become almost obese, ignoring first the hints and then the pleas of her husband and grown children. She remained organically healthy and sound, but developed arthritis in her knees, hips, and other joints, and used this as an excuse to abandon tennis and walking. The less she moved, the heavier she became, and the worse her leg joints became—until finally, she hardly moved at all.

Now in her late seventies, she is almost immobile, unable to travel with her husband as they had always done. She is able to shop only with great difficulty and has become increasingly grumpy and demanding. The quality of Marie's life at this stage is miserable, and the people around her are suffering as a result.

BERT

As a younger man, Bert was more interested in partying than in his health. Although he had an admirable work ethic and a fine family, he lived a careless and dissolute life, ending up an alcoholic. He developed cirrhosis of the liver, resulting in near-fatal internal bleeding. His doctor gave him only weeks to live.

Miraculously, Bert recovered in Alcoholics Anonymous in the nick of time at age forty-four. With his drinking problem behind him, he became interested in health and wellness. He began to eat wholesome and nutritional foods and to do strenuous calisthenics for forty-five minutes each morning. When jogging became a fad in the late 1950s, he became a daily runner, working up to four miles a day. He resumed youthful enthusiasm for skiing, tennis, and sailing. He consciously adopted a positive, accepting, spiritual attitude toward life. He became a responsible, loving husband and father, and resumed a successful career.

Bert continued his second half work life until he turned seventy, when he plunged with zest into an entirely different third half lifework. His levels of health, vigor, and energy are "awesome," in the words of an admiring grandson, who has trouble keeping up. Bert declares, "By the grace of God, I am literally younger today than I was thirty years ago, when I was feeble, helpless, ill, and *old* in my forties."

His wife corroborates this. "We always had a good marriage," she says, "but now it's like a long honeymoon. In his seventies, Bert is as frisky as a colt."

The answer to the "chicken or egg" question is clear: Marie leads a sad, incapacitated life in her older years because she became sedentary at exactly the time she should have increased her physical activity. Bert, who didn't even become interested in wellness until his forties, is a model of health, vigor, and happiness in his older years.

A VIGOROUS LIFESTYLE

The bottom line: to stay active and healthy until the day you die, you need to maintain a vigorous lifestyle. You need to make exercise a part of your daily routine, even when it seems you don't have the time or energy. *Make* the time.

The New York Times reported on a study of seventeen thousand Harvard alumni which found that those who were healthy attributed it to being active. The study also found that moderate exercise throughout adult life is the key to longevity—and that it could "partly counter the death-promoting effects of cigarette smoking, high blood pressure or an inherited tendency toward early death." Regular exercise, the report said, keeps muscles strong and flexible, improves sleep, keeps weight down, improves circulation, leads to a more positive attitude, slows loss of bone mass and improves sex life! Exercising regularly complements good nutrition and slows the aging process. It's another case of the familiar adage, "Use it or lose it."

NO AGE LIMIT ON SEX

Incidentally, as borne out by Bert's wife and the Harvard study, medical experts assure us that there is no upper age limit on an active sex life. A healthy, vigorous body continues to produce the hormones that stimulate interest, and that's all it takes. A diminishing sex life may result from lack of interest or mental worries, but usually not from physical inability. In fact, Dr. David Gutman, a psychologist at Northwestern University, observes that when men retire, they are entering a time when they can be more tender, nurturing, and loving—qualities that may have gotten in the way in their careers. Now these traits can emerge, and men coming home in retirement often "want to recapture the intimacy of their marriage."

One wife of a retiree was frank about it: "The demands of the children took first priority in the earlier years and Sam was so focused on his business. Now he's focused on *me!* We have more time together and more time, period! We've always been in love, but now we seem to spend more time in bed and it's heaven."

But Eda LeShan, author of *It's Better To Be Over The Hill Than Under It,* brings up the other side of sex after sixty. As a psychologist, she gets close to people's intimate lives. She has discovered that it is not true that everyone is, as she puts it, "having a rollicking good time." And many are finding that "you know what" just does not interest them like it once did. They admit to being more interested in just plain cuddling—because the old hormones and gonads don't seem to be as active as they once were. However, many are feeling guilty because of all the stories about remarkable ninety-year-olds "rolling in the hay twice a week." LeShan calls this guilt the "Dr. Ruth Syndrome." And she complains that when we were young, we felt guilty about feeling too sexy. Now that we are older, we are being made to feel guilty because of not feeling sexy enough! As she describes it, our current idea of heaven is not some wild fantasy, but "a hot game of bridge followed by a mushroom pizza."

Referring to the earlier study of Harvard alumni, *The New York Times* columnist Jane Brody offered even more optimistic estimates of how regular, moderate exercise can reverse many of the effects of aging. If you start young enough, Brody said, you may set back your biological clock by twenty-five to forty-five years. She also points out that "You don't have to run marathons to reap the benefits. For the average older person who does little more than rapid walking for a half hour three or four times a week, it can provide ten years of rejuvenation."

SEVEN BASICS FOR A LONGER, HEALTHIER LIFE

The Harvard study recommended seven simple "good habits" that can extend your life expectancy an average of fifteen years. These habits may sound familiar, like the ones your mother tried to teach you at her knee. But save your scorn, because they *work!*

1. Sleep seven to eight hours a night.
2. Don't allow yourself to add more than ten pounds over the normal weight for your height, build, and age.
3. Get moderate aerobic exercise *every day* by walking, or swimming, or participating in active sports.
4. Eat three sensible, nutritious meals per day; eliminate snacks between meals.
5. Don't smoke.
6. Don't drink—or if you do, consume no more than 3 ounces of alcohol per day.
7. Be happily married; married people live longer than single people!

NUTRITION—EATING RIGHT

To the silent generation, the very word "nutrition" was a turnoff. It conjured up pictures of hippies subsisting on brown rice, dried apricots and tofu. But the whole world has turned around in a dizzyingly short time. Just look at restaurant menus, food commercials on television, and almost every item on your supermarket shelves. On a recent plane trip, when we were served a pat of low-fat, no-cholesterol butter substitute we knew that "The Age of Nutrition" had arrived!

Many excellent books on nutrition are available at your public library or bookstores that we will simply touch on the topic here. Suffice it to say, nutrition simply means putting into your body the foods that are good for you and avoiding those which are not. The key is knowing the difference and exercising common sense. If you want to gain vibrant good health and maintain it until the day you die, then start eating right, *now*. It will have an immense effect on the quality of your life in the long run.

LIMIT SUGAR

Scientist Linus Pauling, admittedly a fanatic ahead of his time, once wrote, "I believe if people were to avoid sucrose—hardly ever spoon sugar from the sugar bowl onto anything, avoid sweet desserts except when you're a guest, avoid buying foods containing sugar—they would cut down on the incidence of disease and increase life expectancy. Take a fair amount of vitamins. Stop smoking cigarettes. And you'll have a longer and happier life—more vim and vigor and a better time altogether."

LIMIT FATS

Today, fat, rather than sugar, is the number one bad guy. Because fat—and particularly the wrong *kind* of fat—ends up in the lining of your blood vessels as well as on your waist, it is a major factor in causing hypertension and heart attacks. Even if you are careful, you may end up getting three times as much fat as is good for you—because it's hidden in many of the foods you eat.

Most of the silent generation grew up eating fried foods, creamed dishes, and lots of butter and mayonnaise—but few vegetables and fruits. Back then, potatoes and pasta were thought to be fattening and bad for you, while beef was considered nourishing and even thinning. "Protein diets" were the rage for losing weight.

SOME OTHER DOs AND DON'Ts

Now all that is reversed. Potatoes and pasta (without the butter, sour cream, or cream-based sauces) are considered good for you, because they provide complex carbohydrates, which the body needs. Meat, on the other hand, is out because it's high in the wrong kind of fat. Fried foods, potato chips, and rich ice cream, unhappily, are on the "don't" list. Today's nutrition-conscious younger generation eats lots of fruits, vegetables, and salads, and drinks fruit and vegetable juices in large quantities. A friend of ours says, "Twenty-five years ago, I had trouble finding a store that even carried cranberry juice. Today's supermarkets have whole *sections* devoted not only to cranberry juice in infinite mixtures, but also every other kind of fruit juice imaginable."

WATER, WATER, AND MORE WATER!

Drink six to eight glasses of water a day—not liquids, *water!* Water aids digestion, helps keep your weight down by washing out fats, and helps keep the cells in your bones and skin from drying out. It keeps your urinary system fully functioning and is thought to help prevent incontinence when you become *very* old.

VITAMINS AND MINERALS

Vitamins and minerals serve as catalysts to help build and strengthen the body. While vegetables and fruits are an invaluable source of these elements, don't hesitate to take vitamin and mineral supplements. David Brown says, "I regard [vitamins] the same way as I do religion . . . I take them because their adherents may be right—just as I worship because I don't want to be left out if the religionists are right."

You no doubt have preferences among the foods that are "good for you," as well as "sins" you're reluctant to give up. But as you enter the third half of life, it's time to have the common sense to prefer good health over bad. Learn about nutrition. Listen to the experts. Take responsibility for your own well-being.

Here is a generally accepted list of dos and don'ts:

Don't Overdo:	*Do Consume:*
salt	fish—the oils are beneficial
sugar	a varied diet
coffee and tea	6–8 glasses of water daily
alcohol	less as you age
vitamin doses	
red meat or skin of fowls	
fats—limit intake to monosaturates	

Moderation in all things is still a good rule to go by. The exception is smoking cigarettes. The overwhelming medical evidence is that even a little smoking is bad for you, and those around you. Unless you are bent on self-destruction, quit.

MENTAL HEALTH

Your mental health is as important as your physical health—because most health experts today agree there is a direct correlation between the two. Mental health and physical health do seem to go together, whether you're talking about cancer, heart disease, or, as Miss Adelaide learned in *Guys and Dolls,* the common cold. What you *think* affects how you *feel.* Take Joe Alston, the Wallace Stegner character, who we first discussed in chapter 1.

JOE ALSTON

Joe's depression becomes apparent to his friend and doctor, Ben, during a chat. Ben says to Joe, "You know what you've got? You've got a bad case of the sixties. The sixties are the age of anxiety. You feel yourself on the brink of old age, and you fret. Once you pass your seventieth birthday, all that will clear away. You're like a man with an old car and no place in particular to go. You drive it where you want to, and every day it keeps on running is a gift. If you avoid the killer diseases and keep the degenerative ones under control with a sensible diet and regular exercise . . . you can live nearly forever strictly speaking. There doesn't seem to be any such thing as old age. You can keep chicken tissues alive indefinitely in a nutrient broth."

Joe replies, "You know, it's a funny thing . . . I never had the slightest desire to live in a nutrient broth." Exasperated, Ben says, "You're bored with your garden . . . Whom do you see? Who are your friends?" Ben continues lecturing Joe about getting out more, pointing out that too often "old age is self-inflicted."

WHAT MATTERS MOST IS HOW YOU HANDLE STRESS

Joe exemplifies failure in dealing with the stress of retirement, and the depression that resulted. Ben, who has been troubled with major health problems himself, has transcended them, has stayed involved and vital, and is at peace with life. Remember, retirement ranks sixth among the sixty most stressful experiences—on a par with being jailed or contracting a major disease.

BEATING THE AGE GAME

An article in *The New York Times* by Daniel Goleman reports research which shows that major stress for men often begins in their fifties (sometimes called the "midlife crisis," as discussed in chapter 3). That's when "most people first think of their lives in terms of how much time is left rather than how much time has passed . . . For many, there is a silent despair, a pressing fear of becoming irrelevant in work or marriage, with no real alternative in sight . . . There is a hard time of personal struggle which centers on questions like the value of a marriage or career, or what changes will allow a more meaningful life."

Women in their fifties, on the other hand, are just getting out again after years at home as mothers. Glad to be loose from the demands of home and family, they're eager to enter the world of work and make their mark, which means taking on *outside* demands. Thus they typically are not candidates for major stress or depression. Obviously, this is an inharmonious situation. No wonder current data indicates that most marital trouble in the third half of life involves couples where the wife is working and the husband is not.

These outside demands also can take their toll on people's general health. At her biannual physical checkup, a friend of ours was told her blood pressure had skyrocketed. It was so high the doctor talked of medications, if it didn't go down almost immediately. Upon reflection, she realized how a project she had been working on had been wonderfully enjoyable, yet very stressful because of time pressures and a constant sense of hurry up and wait. She had been driving herself relentlessly for a long time.

Hating the idea of medications and the side effects she had seen in her elderly mother, she decided to try to control her blood pressure herself. She remembered a very good little book by Dr. Herbert Benson, of the Harvard Medical School, called *The Relaxation Response,* which explains the connection between stress and high blood pressure. Finding the book at her local library, she practiced its simple technique, and at the same time, made some diet changes suggested in another book on healing and nutrition. In ten days, her blood pressure was back to normal and the doctor dismissed her.

Some Simple and Healthy Ways to Handle Stress:

· Acknowledge your concerns and worries about the future, and prioritize them in order of urgency and importance.
· Allow *all* the things on your mind to surface. Don't stuff them in some dark recess, thinking they'll go away. They won't.
· Don't harbor anger or resentments. They can't harm the person you're resenting, but they are poison for you.
· Deal with those things you can change—and set aside the things you can't.
· Talk things out with your spouse. He or she will usually welcome the intimacy of sharing.
· If you are single, talk things out with someone. Don't try to carry your burdens alone.

In another *Times* piece, Jane Brody reported a study by the University of Nebraska of 256 elderly people. Those having close "confiding relationships had better immune function and lower levels of cholesterol and uric acid in their blood." Likewise another larger study in Alameda County, California, "showed that those with many social ties—a spouse and friends—had significantly lower death rates. Women in the study who lacked social support were more likely to get cancer, and men in the study who developed cancer died sooner if they were socially isolated."

DEPRESSION

Depression is not uncommon in the third half of life. Dr. Sanford I. Finkel, writing in an AARP Bulletin, defines clinical depression and says that first of all, a person has to have been in a "down mood" for several weeks, unable to find enjoyment in anything, perhaps even taking to bed, unwilling to get up. In addition, he or she needs to show four of the following eight symptoms:

1. sleep problems,
2. diminished interest in anything,
3. guilt,
4. low energy,
5. poor concentration,

6. poor appetite,
7. psychomotor agitation or retardation,
8. suicidal ideas.

When any four of these occur, a person should seek help.

Depression apparently can be caused by any number of things, including a physical imbalance, such as low thyroid or low levels of essential vitamins and minerals. In women, menopause may be a factor. And in anyone, unresolved emotional issues such as old hurts, anger, fears, or feelings of guilt can trigger depression.

If you are suffering from stress, depression, or any other mental problems that are interfering with your enjoyment of life, consider therapy. While the silent generation typically has attached a stigma to therapy—equating it with mental institutions and straightjackets —their children grew up in an era when the need for and benefit of occasional therapy is commonly accepted.

A Little Therapy Can Make a Big Difference

Therapy is actually just talking to someone who's able to be objective. It provides an opportunity to talk about yourself and your personal issues with someone who gives you full attention, without expecting anything of you in return. It's a one-way relationship. Think of a therapist as a sounding board whose purpose is to give you the freedom to talk yourself out. You will probably discover parts of yourself that you didn't even know existed—negative messages that may be holding you back as well as untapped power needing to be expressed.

A word of caution: Objectivity is critical in a therapist. So don't try to use a friend for "kitchen therapy." Choose a trained professional. Incidentally, they may call themselves a psychiatrist, a psychologist, or a therapist, depending on their credentials.

Frederick Buechner, in his book *Telling Secrets,* beautifully sums up the psychological catharsis that takes place in good therapy:

> *We cannot undo our old mistakes or their consequences any more than we can erase old wounds we have both suffered and inflicted. But through the power that memory gives us to think, feel, and imagine our way back through time, we can at long last*

*finally finish with the past — in the sense of removing its power
to hurt us and other people and to stunt our growth as human
beings.*

*The sad things that happened long ago will always remain
part of who we are, just as the glad and gracious things will, too.
But instead of being a burden of guilt, recrimination and regret
that make us constantly stumble, even the saddest things can
become a source of wisdom and strength for the journey that still
lies ahead . . . Memory makes it possible for us both to bless the
past, even those parts of it that we have always felt cursed by,
and also to be blessed by it . . . I think [this] is what forgiveness
of sins is all about — the interplay of God's forgiveness of us and
our forgiveness of God — and of each other.*

FORGETFULNESS AND ALZHEIMER'S

A vast amount of misinformation has sprung up in recent years
around forgetfulness, senility, and Alzheimer's disease in older people. Some forgetfulness is normal at any age, but when it occurs in
an older person, he or she thinks in a panic, "Good gracious, I must
be getting Alzheimer's." It is true that in your sixties, seventies, and
eighties, your mental processes may slow a bit, just as your physical
abilities do. For example, it is to be expected that you may forget
names more readily. It is to be expected that you may go into a room
and forget why you went there! An elderly aunt of ours confessed, "I
lost my dish cloth the other day, and couldn't find it for the longest
time! Guess where it turned up: in the refrigerator!" But that aunt's
mind remained sharp as a tack till the day she died.

Attitude means so much. If you say ruefully, "I always seem to
draw a blank on Jeff Rhue's name," your prophesy will no doubt be
self-fulfilling. But if you say to yourself, "Jeff, Jeff, you play the bass
viol so beautifully, I'll just hear that instrument in my head when I'm
grasping for your name, and I'll bet I'll remember next time," then
that prophesy also will be self-fulfilling. In chapter 3, we said that the
capacity for memory does *not* decrease with age; instead, it *grows.*
Go back and reread that chapter for the good news about your brain.

Senility is *not* "just old age setting in," but rather a specific condition, or really a number of conditions, that may develop in later years. Senility is characterized by *serious* forgetfulness, constant repeating, confusion, and other kinds of personality and behavioral changes. The important thing to remember is that senility can be caused by malnutrition or emotional problems, and it is often treatable.

The parent of a friend of ours became senile in her early eighties because of irregular and improper eating, heavy dosages of medication, and a lack of activity in her life. They decided to take her into their own home and halt all medication under a doctor's supervision. Soon she began to eat regularly and ravenously, and became a part of the household routine. In this caring environment, surrounded by love and constant activity, her senility diminished dramatically!

Here's a crude but accurate distinction between a man's forgetfulness and actual senility: If he fails to zip up his fly, that's forgetfulness; if he forgets to zip it *down,* that's senility.

Alzheimer's, on the other hand, is a definite disease that causes changes in the nerve cells of the outer layer of the brain, and ultimately destroys large numbers of these cells. Tragically, Alzheimer's disease is neither treatable nor reversible, so far. But neither is it inevitable! In fact, even among the very elderly, most people do not suffer any significant mental impairment. And of those who do, only half suffer from Alzheimer's disease. So think positively, stay active, and keep your mind fit by constantly learning new things. Remember: Use it or lose it!

BODY, MIND, AND SPIRIT

Ever since the Middle Ages, scientists and philosophers have held the view that each person consists of three separate parts: body, mind, and spirit. That is still valid, except now it is known that the three parts are interrelated. Without question, the state of your mind and spirit affects the condition of your body.

Cancer, cardiovascular disease, asthma, allergies, arthritis, alcoholism, and depression are now called "stress disorders." They have been found to be associated with certain personality types and often can be traced to stressful experiences. Today these stress disorders have replaced infectious diseases as *the* major health problems.

In the 1970s, Dr. Kenneth Pellitier said, "If the prevention of pathology is the ultimate goal of the healing profession, then health practitioners and laymen alike need to address themselves to the entire person—in relation to his or her total environment . . . Since the early 1960s, the enormous incidence of stress-related chronic conditions, and the increasing awareness of the importance of emotional and psychological states have helped *reinstate the psychosomatic perspective in the causes and relief of disease.*"

David Brown, in his *The Rest of Your Life is the Best of Your Life,* says, "Stay calm and don't overreact to petty crises. They're the worst. Don't try to win every argument. Lose some. Winning may shorten your life. It's not necessary always to be on time, or flagellate yourself when you are late. May Robson, active in films in her eighties, attributed her endurance to 'not rushing.' Don't try to see everything or everybody. In Noel Coward's later years he observed, 'People are always telling me about something I have just missed. I find it very restful.' Reduce stress by diminishing expectations. Accept the limits . . . Be loose. Do your best but not your utmost. You will achieve more by cultivating serenity and poise. Pace yourself."

If you are serious about following the advice gathered in this chapter, *beginning now,* you will have a sound basis for health and wellness in your third half of life, as well as your old age. What more could anyone ask?

QUESTIONS ABOUT YOUR HEALTH AND WELLNESS

- Am I satisfied with my fitness? Am I worried at some level about getting old and decrepit? Am I willing to take charge of my life and do something about it?
- Do I eat properly? Do I have good health habits that I am committed to?
- What kinds of exercise do I like—walking one to two miles a day; running twenty to thirty minutes, three times weekly; cycling thirty minutes every other day; swimming twenty to thirty minutes every other day; tennis, golf, or downhill skiing; cross country skiing; rowing twenty to thirty minutes three times a

week; aerobic dancing (and related activities); gardening? What physical activities am I committed to doing?

- Am I overweight from eating too much? Am I smoking at all? Drinking too much? Can I change? Do I need special help from Smokers Anonymous, Alchoholics Anonymous, Weight Watchers? Is it important enough to me to make that effort? Do I realize that I alone am responsible for my condition and what happens later on?
- Am I a little depressed now that I think about it? Should I get a few sessions of therapy?
- Am I willing to go for optimum health in order to enjoy my life to the fullest as long as I live?

PART THREE

YOUR MONEY

In the second half of your life, you've been launching your children into their world of independence and building your nest egg.

These important years are a pathway to freedom. Not freedom from work, but freedom to work in a way that your heart knows is right. Not freedom from learning, but freedom to acquire the knowledge and skills that bring you joy. Not the false freedom of undirected leisure, but the freedom of a life in which leisure is the companion to learning and work.

It is difficult to achieve such a life without careful planning, self-exploration, trial and error. It is almost impossible to achieve it without money.

Conventional wisdom about money and the third half years has changed radically in the last two decades. In the past, the emphasis was on *preserving your assets*. Today, we're much more focused on *preserving quality of life*—and doing it over a long span of years.

This section, written by Shelley Freeman, a financial services expert, outlines strategies and concepts that are essential to preserving the quality of your life, so that you may pursue your new freedom. We say "outline" because, in fact, whole books have been written on the subjects we're about to cover here in a few pages.

BEATING THE AGE GAME

Our objective is not to chart a detailed road map of the financial journey you must take. Rather, it is to alert you to some of the roadblocks and potholes. To give you the knowledge to undertake the trip with confidence. You should, of course, study this subject further and employ the services of financial advisors whom you select with great care.

Without a doubt, it is never too early to start long-term financial planning.

14

Making Your Financial Plans

Studies have shown that people in the third half have two major concerns:

· Outliving their financial resources.
· Becoming a burden to others because of ill health.

This chapter is devoted to helping you discover ways of preventing either concern from becoming a fact of life.

THE THREE GREATEST THREATS TO YOUR FINANCIAL QUALITY OF LIFE

The three greatest threats to your financial security are forces you cannot control, so you must observe how they behave and adjust your activities accordingly. These threats are: inflation, taxes, and health care costs.

INFLATION

Many people are unaware of the tremendous power inflation has to erode the value of their money. Most of us came of age in a time when inflation was less rampant. Perhaps many of us did not even know what it was. During the 1950s, for example, inflation was approximately 2% per year. Which meant that the value of a dollar in 1950 declined, by 1960, to 82 cents.

BEATING THE AGE GAME

Today, many people accept an annual inflation rate of 4–5% as normal, or "moderate." But, if inflation averages 4.5% during this decade, a 1990 dollar will decline in value to only 64 cents by the year 2000!

Let's look at this appalling statistic another way. If you've estimated that you will need an annual income of $50,000 to achieve the lifestyle you want, then in ten years, assuming this same "moderate" rate, you will need $77,648. In twenty years, make that $120,586. And in thirty, it's an astronomical $187,266.

As this book was being completed, the news media was reporting further declines in the rate of inflation—down to the 3% range. So let's calculate what a rate of 3% does to that $50,000 in ten years. It goes up to $67,196. And in twenty years, it climbs to $90,306.

But take heart. While you can't stop inflation, there are steps you can take to nullify its effects. We'll discuss that in more detail in the chapters ahead.

TAXES

Unlike inflation, taxes rank high on our awareness level. While tax laws have changed frequently in recent years, there still are significant benefits granted to Americans who are saving for their future years, or who are already in their third-half years. The chief point here is the double benefit to be gained from putting your funds in such retirement plans as IRAs, Keoghs, and 401(k)s.

The first benefit is that money placed in such plans may be *tax deductible* (IRA rules vary, according to individual circumstances). Income taxes on withdrawals are deferred until you remove the money, which you can do without penalty after age 59½, but which you need not begin to do until age 70½.

The second benefit is that the returns on your investment are not taxed until you withdraw your money. This benefit is called *tax-deferred compounding*. This chart shows you its power.

Two investments, each of $10,000, each paying 8% annually over periods of 10, 20, and 30 years: with investment A, taxes are paid each year; with investment B, earnings compound tax-free and are not paid until the funds are withdrawn.

A word of caution about "tax-free" investing. While just about

HOW $10,000 WILL GROW IN
TAXABLE AND TAX-DEFERRED
INVESTMENTS, EACH EARNING 8%

Years	Investment A Taxed Each Year At 28% Rate	Investment B Tax Deferred Until Withdrawal
10	$17,507	$18,344
20	30,650	36,359
30	53,659	75,251

every expert in the world enthusiastically endorses investments in IRAs, Keoghs, and 401(k)s, they do not automatically endorse every investment product that has a tax-deductible or tax-deferred compounding feature.

It's not our intention here to discuss various investment vehicles, such as life insurance, annuities, or municipal bonds. Every investment option has both advantages and drawbacks, which you must understand and weigh in light of your own needs and plans. Sometimes a taxable investment may serve your situation better than one that sounds enticing because it has a "tax-free" feature. Always study the fine print and seek the advice of a trustworthy expert.

HEALTH CARE COSTS

In recent years, the cost of health care has climbed at 12% a year — almost three times the rate of inflation. We all know of families whose resources were depleted by a serious illness or long-term care in a nursing home. Medicare does not cover many of these costs. Another government program, Medicaid, will — but only after family savings are exhausted. If you don't want that to happen, you need a long-term care alternative (see chapter 17).

STRATEGIES

Now that you have a better idea of the three forces that threaten the financial quality of your life, let's examine the strategies to protect yourself against them.

IDENTIFY AND QUANTIFY YOUR GOALS

The nature of the life you want to lead will indicate the financial support you require. To make a realistic financial plan, you must clarify and list your lifestyle goals. Responding to the questions that conclude each chapter in Part II will help do this. Then, through self-examination and research, you can begin to estimate the cost associated with the life you want to lead.

This is an important and complex process, and reading this book is only one step. Guidelines for determining how much money you will need to maintain your present standard of living after retirement range from 40 percent to 80 percent of current income (see chapter 15). But what value are these guidelines when you may be inspired to create a whole new way of living?

If this is your dream, you must identify your goals. Develop a plan for reaching them. Apply a budget to that plan—and you must do it in writing. So sharpen your pencil and start creating your future.

THE FINANCIAL IMPORTANCE OF PAID WORK

You know by now how we feel about work. We think it's essential. Being engaged in a productive activity, even for little or no pay, gives meaning and direction to your life and bestows physical, psychological, and spiritual benefits.

Continuing paid work into your post-career years can make a tremendous contribution to your financial health as well. We don't mean necessarily a full-time job at your former salary with your former headaches. We mean a task you enjoy, despite the fact it may pay significantly less than you received during your peak earning years. We mean postponing the static existence of the traditional "retirement" indefinitely while you make the process of earning income part of a personally rewarding life.

Clearly, a trend has begun toward working and earning later in life. For years, the trend had been in the other direction—with people retiring at ever younger ages. Now that trend is reversing. The percentage of people between fifty-five and sixty-four who are working and earning is rising. Likewise, the percentage of people aged fifty-five and over (and sixty-five and over) who are working part time is also increasing.

Let's look at some of the financial implications of earning real gold during your golden years.

- If you continue to work through your sixties, you may be able to leave your assets untouched in a retirement IRA or another savings plan where they will continue to benefit from tax-deferred compounding. You needn't withdraw a cent until your seventy-first year.
- If you are sixty-two to sixty-four, you may earn up to $7,680 per year (1993 figure) and still collect full Social Security. For every $2.00 you earn over that amount, you will receive $1.00 less from Social Security. For those who are aged sixty-five to sixty-nine, the maximum before deductions is $10,560, and $1.00 is deducted for every $3.00 you earn over that amount.

  Thus, a couple aged sixty-five, both of whom qualify for maximum Social Security payments, could each earn $10,560 from a part-time job while receiving about $13,000 a year each from Social Security. That's an annual income of over $47,000 — before you have disturbed one penny of interest or dividends from your investments.

  (To find out what your Social Security benefit will be, call (800) 772-1213 and ask for form SSA-7004. It's also known as the Personal Earnings and Benefit Estimate Statement [PEBES]. The form will be sent to you, and you must fill it out and send it back to receive your estimate.)
- Another alternative is to postpone taking Social Security until you are seventy, when you will receive your full benefit, no matter how much money you make. And your benefit will be larger than it would have been if taken earlier.
- If you continue to work through your sixties and seventies and you may wish to continue contributing to a retirement plan (although not to an IRA after 70½), this will enable you to enjoy both tax deductions and tax-deferred compounding.

Not surprisingly, paid work is not only good for your health, it's great for your pocketbook. Next, we'll take a look at how to manage capital assets.

15

Building Your Wealth

The vast majority of Americans don't know enough about asset management. This is costly ignorance. On one hand, it forces many to choose investments that are too conservative and that pay insufficient returns. On the other hand, ignorance of asset management can expose you to improper advice—even fraud—by people who sell financial products.

You simply cannot leave your financial security to others. You must gain enough knowledge to take responsibility for your own future. This chapter can be a starting point.

THREE KEY CONCEPTS

Let's look at three key concepts that will help you understand personal asset management. These are activities that go on throughout your life. They are overlapping and continuous—like three "balls" you must learn to juggle and keep in the air at all times if you want to accumulate wealth.

Don't be put off by the word "wealth." It doesn't necessarily mean millions of dollars. As used here, wealth is money that you have been able to set aside to grow through investment. (Wealth = capital assets = personal savings = investments.)

· *Building Your Wealth*
This is the process of accumulating assets and building your nest

egg. For most people, there are three possible sources: you save part of your earnings; your saved earnings earn more money; you inherit money.

· *Preserving Your Wealth*
This is the process of making sure your assets serve you throughout your life and are not eroded by inflation and taxation.

· *Protecting Your Wealth*
This is the process of shielding your assets from losses because of illness, disability, or personal liability. And ensuring that what you own will pass on to those you designate, without being drained by estate taxes.

As was previously stated, these are concurrent and overlapping concepts. Asset management is a continually changing process, not a fixed position. Now let's consider these concepts step by step.

STEP 1: IDENTIFY YOUR NEEDS

Your wealth is made up of your accumulated assets, including your house, that you will depend upon to fund the third half of your life. Wealth is like a reservoir from which resources flow to make your lifestyle possible.

That's why you must take certain steps to see that the reservoir is sufficiently full. You will only know what is sufficient for you by identifying your lifestyle goals and estimating the financial support they will require.

Because every person's situation is different, a broad "rule of thumb" is being used here to determine requirements for retirement income. The chart below, which is based on the previously cited guideline of 40 percent to 80 percent of current annual income, gives you some examples. It's offered here to illustrate the importance of working out the figures for yourself.

STEP 2: IDENTIFY YOUR RESOURCES

There are five potential sources of income from personal savings: (1) a company pension; (2) IRAs or other individual savings plans; (3) investments; (4) Social Security; (5) other assets, such as your home. To plan ahead, compare your needs to the total annual income you

HOW MUCH WILL YOU NEED?

Current Salary		"Third Half" Requirement
$50,000	× 60%	$30,000
	× 80%	$40,000
$70,000	× 50%	$35,000
	× 70%	$49,000
$90,000	× 40%	$36,000
	× 60%	$54,000

can expect from your resources. The table below provides a simple illustration of how to assess whether your resources will meet your needs.

By following these samples, you can fill in your own data. Based on the chart, or better yet, using your own detailed analysis of your lifestyle objectives, fill in your target requirement on line 2. Obtain, or calculate, the data for lines 3 thru 7. Do you come out like sample A or sample B? Do you have enough resources? Do you need to bridge the gap? If you have enough, proceed to the next chapter, "Preserving Your Wealth." If you need to bridge a gap, read on.

HOW TO ASSESS YOUR THIRD-HALF RESOURCES

		Samples	
		A	B
1)	Enter current salary	$60,000	$60,000
2)	Target requirement @ 60%	$36,000	$36,000
Income Sources			
3)	Company Pension	$15,000	$10,000
4)	IRA/401(k), etc.	5,000	4,000
5)	Investments	10,000	4,000
6)	Social Security	10,000	10,000
7)	Other ___?___	$5,000	$2,000
8)	Total cash before taxes (add lines 3 thru 7)	$45,000	$30,000
9)	Estimated income taxes	3,000	2,000
10)	Net cash income available	$42,000	$28,000
Net Availability			
11)	Extra cash available (subtract line 2 from 10)	$6,000	
12)	Extra cash needed (subtract line 10 from 2)		($8,000)

STEP 3: BRIDGE THE GAP

Many options are available to people who find their resources insufficient to fund the lifestyle they have chosen. Because these options are often used in combinations, weighing the possible implications can become complex and confusing. It's usually helpful in this situation to have a trusted financial advisor who, with the help of a computer program, knows how to manipulate all the possible scenarios.

Chances are your advisor will know of imaginative solutions other clients have employed. Here are several to consider:

- *Reexamine your goals* to see what you can reasonably give up. There is so much joy available in life that giving up a few possessions or experiences may not be a great loss. Look again carefully to discover what is really important.
- If you are still working full time, *accelerate your savings.* Aggressive savings now can reward you for years into the future. One of the best ways to do this, if it's available, is to fund your 401(k) to the maximum. Contributions from your employer accelerate the savings even more.
- *Plan to work longer or to engage in part-time work* during your third half. As you know, we think work is central to a fully realized life. There's no reason you shouldn't receive money for it. As long as you're working (up to age 70½), you can continue tax-advantaged savings for your later years. Continuing to earn money throughout your sixties and into your seventies can have enormous benefits in terms of financial security and a more luxurious lifestyle. It also can do wonders for your mental and physical health.
- *Adjust your investment program to seek higher returns.* The only way to get higher returns is to accept more risk. But many Americans are under-invested because of an unreasonable fear of reasonable risk. We discuss this in the next chapter, "Preserving Your Wealth." This is not to suggest you put your life savings into wheat futures. Rather, that you examine the way your assets are allocated to see if a greater return is possible—without costing you any sleep.
- *Use your home as a resource.* You may be able to sell it, pocket

the gains without paying taxes, and buy a less expensive place. Tax laws permit people over fifty-five to sell a house and pay NO taxes on the first $125,000 in profit. You may do that only once.

There are circumstances where a home equity loan—in which you borrow against the value that has built up in the house— might make sense.

And then there are reverse mortgages. Here you borrow against the house but receive a check each month. You don't actually sell the house, so you may continue to live there as long as you want. The account is settled when you die or get rid of the house.

Another strategy is to sell your house to your children, hold their mortgage, and then rent it from them. You receive their down payment and monthly mortgage check. They receive a monthly rental check from you, plus the tax advantages of owning a rental property.

Your home is a precious asset in more ways than one. Obviously, none of these strategies should be undertaken without careful examination of all options. But they have proven effective and appropriate in bridging the gap for many people.

· *Dip into your principal.* You can't take it with you—but no law says you have to leave it all to someone else. The kicker here is that you're never certain how long you'll need the principal to last. But there are money management strategies that allow you to prudently tap your principal to assure a comfortable life. As you might imagine, this approach is usually employed very late in life.

16

Preserving Your Wealth

In the previous chapter, we introduced the image of the reservoir. It represents those financial (or capital) assets that must nourish you throughout your third half of life. So far, we've talked about deciding how large your reservoir should be and how to fill it up. Now let's talk about preserving it from evaporation, replenishing it, and keeping it as full as possible even while you are drawing on it.

Your twin enemies are taxes and inflation, but especially inflation. If you need a reminder of the enormous power of inflation to evaporate your assets, refer to chapter 14.

The only way you can protect your reservoir from inflation is to invest your resources so they grow equal to, or faster than, inflation. (We are going to bypass the idea of your continuing to work. By now you know how we feel. And these investment principles apply in any event.)

THE COST OF INVESTMENT IGNORANCE

Most experts feel that Americans, as a whole, are woefully poor investors. We have a tendency to entrust such decisions to others without really understanding what's at stake. And we tend to invest much too conservatively for our own good.

When forced to select an investment, Americans often opt for the safest choice which is usually the one paying the lowest returns. Putting all your third-half money into the safest investment can cost you many thousands of dollars over the years.

For several years now, people in financial services have remarked with alarm how employees with company-sponsored 401(k) savings plans manage their own money. Given the choice, the majority of Americans consign their funds to guaranteed investment contracts, which, as the name indicates, pay a "guaranteed" rate of interest. The problem is that the interest rate is often low.

What these employees should be doing, experts say, is putting some of their funds in investments that, with slightly greater risk, have the potential to pay higher returns. If we don't do this, our investments may not outpace inflation and we may find in the third half, that we're scratching to survive—unnecessarily, simply because we don't understand the nature of risk and the basics of diversified investing.

THE PYRAMID OF RISK

There is no such thing as a risk-free investment. It's just that investments bear different kinds and degrees of risk.

Most of us are no strangers to financial risks. One risk we all recognize: that we might lose some or all of our money. But there are other risks, too. In the stock market, for example, volatility is a common risk—values fluctuate and you might buy or sell at the wrong time. In the municipal bond market, there's a risk that you'll get your money back before you want—because the bond issuer will decide to pay off its debt early, leaving you with the problem of having to reinvest it.

Generally, investors who are willing to accept certain kinds of market risks have the potential to receive greater rewards. Stocks of "emerging growth" companies, for example, may seem relatively inexpensive. They may not gain value for years—if ever. "Junk bonds," on the other hand, pay high interest rates to reward the investor for the risk of default.

Here are some examples of risks that are commonly associated with an over-cautious investment strategy:

- *Inflation risk* is the concern that an ever-increasing cost of living will diminish the value of your savings.
- *Interest-rate risk* may be defined as leaving your money in low-

yielding investments, even as rates decline, which typically forces you to live on less income.

· *Opportunity risk* refers to the chance that, through ignorance or fear, you will avoid good opportunities—such as the stock market during much of the 1980s.

We're not suggesting that you take unreasonable risks with your capital. Rather, you should examine the nature of risk to see what your risk tolerance is. Most people in their fifties and sixties describe themselves as "conservative" investors. But what does conservative really mean? For some, it's a savings account or certificates of deposit. For others, it's treasury bonds or a stock mutual fund.

Consider the investment risk pyramid on page 160.

As you can see, there are a number of moderate-risk, conservative investments that offer significantly higher returns than the safest alternatives. After seeing the alternatives arranged this way, with their risks and rewards in perspective, ask yourself how comfortable you'd be with some of your capital assets invested in the various categories.

If you are wondering if you should be in the stock market, the answer from the experts is unanimous: YES. Some portion of your holdings—probably throughout your life—should be invested in stocks. The reason is that over time, stocks consistently outperform all other investment alternatives. How much you should invest in the stock market and how you do it is something only you can decide after careful study and professional advice.

We stress here that you must be comfortable with your investment portfolio. Your investments should help you sleep at night, not keep you awake with worry. You invest to live; you don't live to invest.

THE DIVERSIFIED PORTFOLIO

Diversification is a basic investment rule followed by all professional investors. It's this simple: don't put all your eggs in one basket. You should spread them among different categories of financial assets and among different securities in each of those categories.

Professionals, for example, hold stocks in different companies and

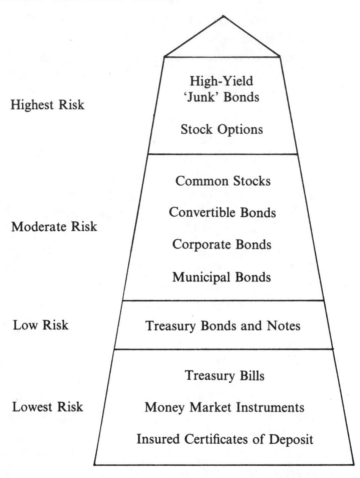

Highest Risk — High-Yield 'Junk' Bonds / Stock Options

Moderate Risk — Common Stocks / Convertible Bonds / Corporate Bonds / Municipal Bonds

Low Risk — Treasury Bonds and Notes

Lowest Risk — Treasury Bills / Money Market Instruments / Insured Certificates of Deposit

industries—and so should you if you plan to invest in individual stocks. If you're going to invest in mutual funds, be certain what the investment objective of the funds is, and consider diversifying among two or three.

Diversification is important because no one can pick a winner every time. In that sense, it's a risk-reduction strategy. But it's also a reward-enhancement strategy. Your goal is not simply to reduce damage from any one investment performing poorly but to reap the gains from good performance in other areas of your portfolio.

ASSET ALLOCATION—A LONG-TERM INVESTMENT STRATEGY

If your investment advisor starts talking to you about "asset allocation," don't fear that you've wandered into a mutual fund's finance committee meeting. Yes, asset allocation is a technique that the big money people use, but it also works for individual investors.

Basically, it's a strategy designed to achieve a specific return on capital over a period of time by placing investments in a variety of categories. Let's say you determine that you need a return on your investment portfolio of 5% above the rate of inflation.

Using a formula based on current market conditions, your assets would be divided among various investments in cash, stocks, and bonds. As the investment pyramid indicates, there are many types of cash, stocks, and bonds—and your funds would be divided among them, depending on how much money you have to invest, what your goals are, and what your risk tolerance is.

As time passed, some sections of your portfolio would do better than others, partly because different investments rise and fall with different market cycles. As market cycles change, your asset allocation formula would change as well. However, your assets would always remain diversified, protected against risk you don't want. And they would remain targeted to achieve the long-term return you identified.

Remember, the goal is not to make a killing, but to support the lifestyle you have envisioned for yourself. Asset allocation, properly conducted, has proven to be a successful and prudent way to go.

COMMON OBJECTIVES OF A DIVERSIFIED PORTFOLIO

Just as your portfolio is composed of a mix of investment types, so is it designed to achieve a mix of objectives. Here are some common ones, briefly defined:

- *Growth.* This is the ability of the capital investment to gain value at a rate that exceeds inflation. But it may not happen in a steady, year-to-year fashion. Growth stocks, for example, aren't expected to "grow" every year, but over a period of five to ten years, they are expected to outpace inflation.

- *Income.* This is the ability of the investment to pay you returns on a regular schedule. Most bonds, for example, pay interest regularly. A growth stock may not pay you anything until you sell it. Annuities don't usually pay income immediately, but at a specific future date.
- *Liquidity.* This describes the ease with which your investment can be turned into cash. Bank money market funds are so liquid you can make withdrawals at automatic teller machines. On the other hand, two thousand acres of farmland is highly illiquid.
- *Safety.* We define safety as the investment's ability to return your principal at any given time. Federally insured certificates of deposit are safe. Mutual funds usually are safer than individual stocks, because they are diversified and professionally managed.

MODEL PORTFOLIOS

To show you how asset allocation strategies change according to circumstances, three model portfolios have been developed. Notice the relationship between asset allocations, the clients' objectives, and their risk tolerance.

We've made some arbitrary assumptions to illustrate a basic point: how the asset allocation formula might change according to age, financial goals, and investment priorities. The allocations shown here seemed appropriate for today's financial markets. They may no longer be valid by the time you read this.

Now, let's look at three stages in life. To begin, assume total investment assets are $300,000; assume a "moderate" investment risk tolerance; and assume a target investment income at least 5 percent above inflation.

A word of caution: This scenario is not intended to be a guideline —it simply reflects one possible investment philosophy. For example, if your third-half resources can produce more than adequate income to meet your lifestyle goals, and if you are trying to increase capital values to benefit your heirs, you might not want to shift from moderate to conservative, low-risk investments.

Some experts recommend a conservative approach when your circumstances are "tight." However, the issue of balancing inflation will always present the main challenge in preserving your capital wealth.

EXAMPLE "A"
AGE 53 WITH 12 MORE FULL-TIME CAREER YEARS

Investment priorities:
1) Capital growth
2) Tax deferral/reduction
3) Liquidity
4) Current income

Asset Allocation	Amount	Percent
Growth-oriented investments	$165,000	55
Tax-free fixed income	120,000	40
Tax-free money market funds	15,000	5

Notes: Slightly more than half of this portfolio is oriented toward growth investments, such as common stocks, which, over the long run, tend to produce the greatest "total" return—that is, increased capital value and increasing dividend payouts. The fixed-income investments provide a steady interest flow while the money market funds are a source of ready cash.

EXAMPLE "B"
AGE 60 WITH 5 MORE YEARS TO GO

Investment priorities:
1) Capital growth
2) Tax deferral/reduction
3) Current income
4) Liquidity

Asset Allocation	Amount	Percent
Tax-free fixed income	$150,000	50
Growth-oriented investments	135,000	45
Tax-free money market funds	15,000	5

Notes: Here, the allocation remains strongly oriented toward growth because "B" is expected to live many more years. At the same time, the allocation has become slightly more conservative and is geared toward producing fixed returns at predictable times. More than half of the portfolio is in tax-free investments.

EXAMPLE "C"
AGE 70 AND NOW IN THE THIRD HALF

Investment priorities:

1) Current income
2) Liquidity
3) Capital growth
4) Tax-deferral/reduction

Asset Allocation	Amount	Percent
Tax-free fixed income	$195,000	65
Growth-oriented investments	75,000	25
Tax-free money market funds	30,000	10

Notes. Over the past 17 years, the emphasis has shifted toward a predictable, steady flow of income that, we may assume is financing our investor's lifestyle. Concerns about growth have not disappeared; "C" still has many years ahead. Tax reduction is still a factor.

17

Protecting Your Wealth

Now that you understand how to manage your capital assets for proper growth to nourish your lifestyle, it's time to look at strategies for protecting your wealth. By this is meant setting up systems to prevent outside forces from siphoning off your assets—forces such as natural catastrophes, long-term illness, and taxes.

Protecting your wealth also involves making provisions to ensure your heirs and beneficiaries receive it. This aspect of managing your assets is the most personal and most complicated. Your financial advisors need to understand the subjective *you*. What follows are a few tips to help you identify major issues.

INSURANCE: THE FIRST LINE OF DEFENSE

As you grow older, your insurance needs change. It is assumed that your home, car, and personal liability are properly insured and turn our attention to four other forms of insurance: life, health, disability, and long-term care.

LIFE INSURANCE

A growing number of people in their forties, fifties, and sixties are investing in life insurance today. Why? Because certain life insurance policies can uniquely meet important needs, in addition to providing basic income protection in case of untimely death.

First, Wealth Protection and Estate Planning

The federal government taxes any net estate over $600,000, and the long-term effects of inflation are placing a higher percentage of American families in that category. Life insurance death benefits are immediately available to pay estate taxes, so that the estate value is protected through the purchase of insurance policies.

Furthermore, the proceeds from life insurance "owned" by someone or some entity other than the insured are not included in your estate for federal inheritance tax purposes. You can establish a "life insurance trust" just to own your policies.

In addition to death benefits, many life insurance products provide an attractive investment alternative. Because of tax-deferred compounding features (see chapter 14), money invested in today's policies—particularly variable life insurance that offers investment of cash values in various types of stocks, bonds, and money market funds—can yield competitive rates of return.

Second, Liquidity

Money placed in life insurance cash values also is readily accessible in the event of emergencies by taking out a loan on the policy. This provides a liquidity advantage, and such loans are usually free from federal income taxes.

Third, Death Benefits before You Die

Life insurance policies are now available with a "living needs benefit" feature. Nearly all the value of the death benefit can be paid out in case of a life-threatening disease, organ transplant, permanent confinement in a nursing home, or terminal illness.

A related practice coming into use involves insuring against a specific terminal illness, such as cancer or AIDS. For instance, an outside company might buy the life insurance policy for 60–70% of its death benefit. That way, the insured receives the money when it's needed, and the company receives the death benefit when the person dies.

Fourth, Large Estates

Some individuals or business owners with taxable estates in excess of $600,000 find life insurance an effective way of assuring that inheritance taxes do not become a burden. This form of insurance is called "second-to-die," and since it's essentially an estate-planning strategy, we'll discuss it later in this chapter.

Given the combination of benefits that life insurance can provide, it is a necessary part of an overall financial plan for many people. Because each person's situation is different, it's prudent to get good advice from a trusted agent or financial planner before making decisions about buying life insurance, particularly those policies intended to meet specialized needs that may arise later on in life.

DISABILITY INSURANCE

If you are counting on earning part of your third-half income, you need disability income insurance. Its purpose is to replace income you lose through injury or illness. The older you get the more you need it, since your odds of getting a disabling illness or injury increase with age. In many cases, it's just as important as life insurance. Of course, the longer you wait the more it costs and many companies won't even offer it at all after age sixty-five.

If you're covered through your job by worker's compensation insurance and incur a work-related injury, or you're on Social Security, you probably would be entitled to some disability pay—but it might not be enough. And if you are between jobs or have just changed employers, you probably aren't covered at all.

We encourage you to take this matter very seriously if income from paid work is essential to your third-half objectives.

HEALTH INSURANCE

The strategy here is to cover any "gaps." For example, there may be gaps in time between your current policy and Medicare, which you are eligible for at age sixty-five if you meet the requirements for Social Security.

Even after Medicare begins, you can expect gaps, this time between what Medicare pays and what your health care costs. Many people in their post-career years are fortunate to have health insurance policies provided by their former employers. However, companies are rapidly curtailing or rescinding such policies, and the likelihood is growing that you will be required to assume more of the cost or receive reduced benefits.

If you're not lucky enough to have a company offer you less expensive group health insurance, you'll have to buy your own. The key, as always, is to understand your needs and stoutly resist any efforts to sell you more protection than you require.

One money-saving tactic is to accept a high deductible—say $1,000 or $2,000—compared to the lower deductibles common in company group policies. This will drive down your annual premium considerably, in effect recovering the deductible through savings you enjoy on the premium.

"Medigap" is the name for a group of federally approved standard insurance policies that help cover costs not covered by Medicare. These costs are many and can be quite large. If you are not covered by a company policy, you should get Medigap coverage, which is available through groups such as the American Association of Retired Persons. Premiums range from about $500 a year up to $1,500, depending on the coverage selected.

You will become eligible for Medicare when you reach age sixty-five, even if you continue to work and do not start taking Social Security benefit payments. (Be sure to sign up *before* your sixty-fifth birthday.)

Even if you have a company policy, you should sign up, because such policies usually assume that Medicare is in place. Company health insurance policies often evolve into a "Medigap" substitution policy and no longer function as your principal protection. When you sign up for Medicare, you automatically will be enrolled in Plan A, which covers hospital bills and other skilled nursing and health care. If you need it, you may also purchase Plan B coverage, which helps with doctor bills and other expenses not covered by Plan A.

LONG-TERM CARE

Most people rely on (or assume they can rely on) family care-givers, either in their own home or a loved one's. Often this works well. For some, however, it's a miserable experience.

One option is a special insurance policy to cover many of the expenses of nursing home care that are not paid by Medicare. Increasingly, financial experts are recommending this insurance, starting at about age sixty-five, for those who can afford it. Otherwise, you may be forced to spend your savings on nursing home care. When your savings are exhausted, you will be covered by Medicaid.

Another long-term care strategy is to enter a "life-care community." Here, you buy an apartment in a facility that is partially a condominium-like community and partially a nursing home. In addition to buying your apartment, you pay a monthly fee that covers meals (if you don't want to cook your own) and other services. These are often attractive options for people aged seventy-five or older who are in relatively good health but want some help or companionship. If long-term nursing care is required later, the facility provides it, often at no incremental cost and often in a separate wing or building. These arrangements can be expensive, but they also can be very comfortable, even luxurious, and offer a great deal of companionship and recreational services.

PUTTING YOUR ESTATE IN ORDER

Estate planning is the process of making certain your assets will be distributed after your death, according to your wishes — and that the expenses of doing so, such as taxes and probate costs, will be kept as low as possible. But such planning can't be left to the last minute, for the simple reason that you never know when the last minute will come. So assume it's coming in six months and prepare now.

Proper estate planning is about much more than money. Surely you'll want those close to you to remember you as a thoughtful, caring person. But if you make no plans, your legacy could be confusion, disharmony, and anger.

Yet it has been estimated that *two-thirds of adult Americans* leave the decisions about their worldly wealth and possessions to strangers! If you die without a will, the state will divide your assets among family members, according to a formula that very well may not reflect your wishes. If you have no blood relatives, the state will keep the money. Your friends, your church, your synagogue, and your college will receive nothing. Chances are, your lack of planning could cause trouble among your family members.

Here are some key estate-planning steps you should consider. You will need expert help in making the right decisions about each of these matters. Do learn as much as you can from reading, but don't rely solely on a book or pamphlet to develop your plans.

A WILL

A proper will enables you to designate who is to receive your assets and possessions, and in what proportion or quantity. You also designate an executor who has the responsibility to make this happen. And you open the matter to probate, the process by which the state oversees what is being done. Probate is administered by the government—which means it is open to review by the public and may be subject to long delays.

A LIVING TRUST

In recent years, millions of Americans have avoided probate by establishing a living trust, rather than a will, and naming a trustee to do the same work as the executor. While a living trust is a private matter and may be a quicker process than probating a will, financial experts advise that the choice between them is a highly individual matter. If you decide to pursue a living trust, be certain to get professional help. All assets you own must be transferred to the trust and failure to do this properly could invalidate all your plans.

DESIGNATING BENEFICIARIES

A good deal of what will happen to your financial assets is, or can be, built into the system. Life insurance, IRAs, Keoghs, and other pension plans require that you designate beneficiaries. Any property you own jointly (with right of survivorship) with your spouse, such as a home or savings account, goes automatically to the surviving spouse. Other property you own jointly with another person may be passed, in the ownership contract, to that person.

THE LIVING WILL

This is a written expression of your desire not to prolong your life by artificial treatment when there is no hope for recovery. State laws on living wills vary. To strengthen your document, it is recommended that you authorize someone to act on your behalf as a "health-care proxy" or "health-care power of attorney" to see that your wishes are carried out.

POWER OF ATTORNEY

This document authorizes someone else to act on your behalf if you become incapacitated. There are a number of forms, granting a range of powers. A *durable* power of attorney is the most sweeping; it gives someone complete authority to act for you in all matters, if you become mentally ill, senile, or suffer a brain-damaging accident. Other forms grant limited or specific powers. Powers of attorney should be renewed from time to time. Again, state laws vary.

ASKING SOMEONE TO ACT ON YOUR BEHALF

So far, a very serious subject has been skipped blithely over—selecting the person who will act as your executor, trustee, or power of attorney. Choosing fiduciaries is one of the most difficult decisions about estate planning. Should you choose a family member, a friend, your lawyer, a bank, or some other institution? How many fiduciaries do you want? And what about successor fiduciaries in the event someone is unable to serve? You need to resolve these questions with your family and attorney.

Only a moment's thought tells you that these tasks can be time-consuming, difficult, and even agonizing. Most people select a spouse, an heir, or a trusted friend. Since it's possible they may die or become incapacitated before the job is finished, it's often recommended that you name coexecutors. For greater assurance, the coexecutor could be a professional associated with a firm or institution—for example, a lawyer, accountant, or banker. That way, even if something happened to the individual, the organization would carry out your wishes.

INFORM THE PEOPLE CONCERNED

Once you have made your plans and selected an executor or trustee, you'll need to inform others. Your executors, spouse, or others close to you need to know where to find your will, your records, your life insurance policies, your safe deposit key, and any wishes you have for your funeral or burial.

AVOIDING ESTATE TAXES

Estate taxes can be either a nonproblem or a nuisance. In the former instance, no federal taxes are due on a net estate valued at $600,000 or less. Further, any inheritance of any size that passes to your spouse is not taxable. After that, the complexitities begin.

If your net estate exceeds $600,000, there are a number of tactics you should consider to not only minimize taxes but to assure an orderly transfer of your wealth. You will want professional help, but here are some key considerations.

OWNERSHIP REVIEW

There are a number of forms of ownership. The most common for spouses is "joint ownership with right of survivorship," which means that the assets pass directly to one spouse when the other dies. You should review all assets to ascertain how they are owned—singly, jointly, in a trust—and make a judgment, with the help of your advisor, about whether the current form of ownership is the most beneficial. A "disclaimer trust" provision in your will actually gives the surviving spouse one year after the death to change the nature of the ownership.

ESTABLISH ONE OR MORE TRUSTS

Trusts, sometimes called unified credit trusts or bypass trusts, allow a husband and wife to shelter up to $1.2 million from estate taxes. Each must have a separate estate valued at $600,000, so this is where it is important to review the nature of ownership.

SECOND-TO-DIE INSURANCE

Often the purpose of this insurance is not to pass on wealth but to provide funds to pay estate taxes on estate assets that otherwise might have to be sold quickly to pay the taxes. This could be a house or a business, for example. The insurance actually covers both the wife and husband, but does not pay policy proceeds until they both have died. The proceeds pay the estate taxes on the business, for instance, by allowing the heirs plenty of time to decide whether to keep it going or look for a buyer.

ENJOY THE PLANNING PROCESS

Over the past four chapters highlights of making your financial plans have been covered. Using these chapters as a checklist, you may find you have much to do—or very little. Either way, do not view the work ahead as drudgery.

Rather, you are taking crucial financial steps toward the freedom you've worked so long to enjoy. With every completed task, you remove concerns and uncertainties that may have been troubling you unnecessarily. So enjoy the process with the knowledge that you are improving the quality of the life you'll live and the legacy you'll leave.

Peace of mind is the reward for those who have their money issues in order.

A CHANGING AMERICA

George Bernard Shaw once said, "A continuous vacation is a good working definition of hell." More and more, people are recognizing the truth of that statement—and revolting in a variety of ways to avoid that kind of hell on earth. After fulfilling their second half responsibilities of raising a family and establishing a financial base sufficient to sustain themselves, they devote themselves to "a work"—something fruitful they can do to help the world at large. By adding this dimension to traditional retirement, they're finding that this stage—which we like to call the third half —of life does not signal the end, but rather, the beginning of a whole new adventure.

Life has never been better. They're having fun using their skills and expertise to the benefit of themselves and others. Their lives have meaning and purpose. Most of all, they are happy, because they feel good about themselves.

This spiritual aspect of life is the focus of Part IV. We'll explore the importance of having a spiritual base and discuss cultural blocks that sometimes prevent people from participating in the quiet revolution as fully as they might like. Government and business need to recognize that this revolution is changing America. Today, people in their second half can, at the very least, look forward to a bright future and perhaps, more importantly, become a vital force in influencing institutional changes that support the revolution under way.

Without question, a new frontier has opened up for mature Americans. The silent generation is quietly and surely pioneering a better way of life—and proving in the process that the third half of life can often be the most beneficial years for themselves and for society.

18

Meaning In Your Life

Having a meaning and purpose in our lives is our number one need. If we don't have any sense of meaning; if we can't point to any purpose of being beyond our . . . self-interest, all the power and prestige and privilege in the world will leave us hollow and incomplete.

—Dr. Ralph Ahlberg

I have frequently seen people become neurotic when they content themselves with inadequate or wrong answers to the questions of life. They seek position, marriage, reputation, outward success or money, and remain unhappy and neurotic even when they have attained what they were seeking. Such people are usually confined within too narrow a spiritual horizon. Their life has not sufficient content, sufficient meaning. If they are enabled to develop into more spacious personalities, the neurosis generally disappears.

—Dr. Carl Jung

I am always happy if I'm working . . . To be fruitful is to be happy. You don't have to feel you've got the tiger by the tail; it's when you can't find the tiger that the agony begins.

—Arthur Miller

THE SPIRITUAL SIDE

The observations of these distinguished men say it all. If you are to have a joyful, productive, fulfilled third half, your life must have *meaning*. Arthur Miller beautifully described what happens when a person has none.

As we said in chapter 13, scientists and philosophers have long held that every person consists of three separate yet interrelated parts: body, mind, and spirit. In that chapter, we dealt with the importance of having a healthy, active body and mind in our older years. And chapter 3, devoted to older growing, explained why there is no reason to expect our minds to decline as age increases. But, as Drs. Ahlberg and Jung have stated so explicitly, all this comes to naught if our physical and mental selves are not undergirded by the spirit.

WHAT DOES IT ALL ADD UP TO?

In a "Peanuts" cartoon, Charlie Brown is lying in bed, wide awake while his dog Snoopy sleeps peacefully at his side. He is saying to himself, "Sometimes I lie awake at night, and I ask, 'What is the meaning of life?'

"Then a voice comes to me that says, *'i* before *e* except after *c.'* "

For many of us, Peanuts creator Charles Schultz cuts close to the bone with this one. We sometimes wonder about the meaning of life and come up as empty as Charlie Brown.

A SENSE OF WELL-BEING

Passages author Gail Sheehy wrote a book entitled *Pathfinders,* based on a three-year study of sixty thousand people representing all strata of society and all parts of the country. They were questioned about their goals, values, experiences, as well as their perceptions of themselves and their feelings of well-being at each stage in their lives. The findings are relevant:

1. Contrary to what might be expected, the largest number of people who had a strong sense of well-being were older.
2. Although both men and women interviewed had expected

things to get worse as they grew older, they discovered that the opposite was true; life was better.

3. Of ten established hallmarks of well-being, *number one was a feeling that their lives had meaning and direction.*

Sheehy sums up by saying, "Well-being registers deep in our unconscious. It is an accumulated attitude, a sustained background tone of equanimity behind the more intense contrasts of daily events, behind even periods of unhappiness."

BEYOND REASON

This same thought is expressed in a very popular meditation book, *Twenty-Four Hours a Day,* published by Hazelden, which says, "The only way to keep calm and sane in this troubled world is to have a serene mind. The calm and sane mind sees spiritual things as the true realities and material things as only temporary and fleeting. That sort of mind you can never obtain by reasoning, because your reasoning powers are limited by space and time. That kind of mind you can never obtain by reading, because other minds are also limited in the same way. You can only have that mind by an act of faith, by making the venture of belief."

Alcoholics Anonymous, which has changed millions of lives, provides a convincing example of the importance of finding meaning in one's life and relying on a power outside oneself. A seldom realized fact is that the AA program, as contained in its famous Twelve Steps, does not tell alcoholics how to stop drinking; instead, it shows them how to live a happy, abundant, productive life without having to escape into the bottle. It is essentially a *spiritual* program. The co-founder of Alcoholics Anonymous was fond of relating how this came about.

THE AA STORY

Rowland Hazard, the scion of a prominent Albany, New York, family, had a drinking problem. In 1932, after trying several "cures" of the day without success, the family sent Rowland across the ocean to the care of world-famous psychiatrist Dr. Carl Jung, in Zurich, Switzerland. After a year there, Dr. Jung summoned Rowland to his study and explained, "We have been trying to bring about a deep psychic change in you, but have been unable to do so. So we are discharging you."

No doubt startled, Rowland asked, "Is there no hope, then?"

Dr. Jung's answer was astonishing, coming from a man of science. "No," he replied, "there is none—except we do know that some people with your problem have recovered if they have had a transforming experience of the spirit." Rowland pressed the doctor as to how or where he might have such an experience, but Jung could only suggest that he try to put himself in an environment where such a thing might happen.

Rowland continued to drink, but somehow came in contact with a religious movement of the time, the Oxford Movement. These people were trying to return to the principles of first century Christianity, including confessing their defects of character, praying regularly, making amends for wrongs they had done to others, and devoting their lives to helping their fellowman. Rowland found his transforming experience of the spirit with the Oxford Movement.

While continuing to attend their meetings in New York, he learned that Ebby Thatcher, a boyhood friend and drinking companion, was in trouble with the law after driving drunk through the front wall of a local residence in Vermont. Rowland, by relating his own experiences, persuaded the judge to parole Ebby to his care. He took him back to New York, where Ebby sobered up.

Ebby, attempting to follow the Oxford Movement's principle of helping his fellowman, remembered his old friend, Bill, then in the last stages of alcoholism. Ebby called on him at his home in Brooklyn, where Bill was drinking himself to death while his wife, Lois, supported him by clerking at Macy's. Ebby tried to convince Bill that his only way out was through a spiritual change—but Bill, an agnostic, wasn't buying it.

Bill went on another wild bender, which landed him in Towns Hospital, a drying-out facility in New York. There Ebby called on him again, repeating his message. And after he left, Bill called out to a God in whom he did not believe—and had a dramatic spiritual experience. He never had another drink, and some months later, carried the same message to a drunken surgeon, Bob, in Akron, Ohio, and AA was born.

The message of hope that Dr. Jung gave to Rowland, who gave it to Ebby, who gave it to Bill, who gave it to Bob, has been repeated millions of times since; it is quite simply that the solution to the alcoholic's problem doesn't lie in restoring his physical health, or changing her thinking (although both *do* occur), but in having a transforming experience of the spirit through which his or her life becomes happy, joyous, and free of the need to escape from reality through alcohol.

Mystic and author Gerald Heard believed that "you can either think your way into right acting, or you can act your way into right thinking." The members of Alcoholics Anonymous are convinced the latter is the way to go. They believe that by taking the actions called for in the Twelve Steps, a person's thinking will straighten out and he or she will have a "spiritual awakening as the result."

PURPOSE IN LIFE

World-renowned psychiatrist Victor Frankl, in his best-selling *Man's Search For Meaning*, states: "[It is] a dangerous misconception . . . to assume that what man needs is equilibrium, a tensionless state [of mind]. What man actually needs is . . . striving and struggling for some goal worthy of him; not the discharge of tension at any cost, but the call of a meaning waiting to be fulfilled by him . . ."

How to Find It

Frankl suggests we can find meaning in life through any of three different avenues: (1) by engaging in some work or activity that is meaningful; (2) by experiencing meaning through appreciation of nature, art, or love; (3) by suffering. A survivor of a World War II concentration camp, Frankl believes that the thing which most helped him survive was his wife's image. At times when death seemed almost certain, he says, "I heard her answer me, saw her smile, her encouraging look. I saw the truth as it is set into song by so many poets and proclaimed by so many thinkers—the truth that love is the highest goal to which we can aspire." He also found meaning in life through the suffering he endured in the camp.

Many British who lived through the London blitz see it now as perhaps the richest, most rewarding period in their lives. Because they pitched in and worked together for the common good even at the risk of their lives, they found real meaning for themselves.

Stories abound of "foxhole conversions" by people who found meaning in their lives in moments of peril. Sometimes the opposite occurs.

A favorite story of a couple we know in the third half of life concerns a man who professed vehemently to be a nonbeliever in God or prayer. When asked why, he claimed that the one time he had *really* prayed for God's help in a desperate situation, the help was not forthcoming.

> *"I was a bush-pilot in the Arctic at the time," he related. "One day my engine conked out and I had to make a crash landing in the Arctic snow fields, miles from anywhere. I broke my leg in the crash and couldn't move. It looked like curtains for me, so I prayed as hard as I knew how for God to get me out of the fix I was in. Well, he never answered me."*
>
> *"But you're here," said his listeners.*
>
> *"Yeah," he said. "About a half hour later, a pair of Eskimos came over the hill with a sled and rescued me. But it didn't have anything to do with God!"*

When some unexpected blessing befalls the people we heard the story from, one will turn to the other and say, "Another pair of Eskimos just came over the hill!"

In the article about Liz Carpenter, mentioned in chapter 11, she offers this advice:

> *Meaning in your life isn't just handed to you, as a wayward motorist might be provided with a set of directions. You give life meaning through the commitments you make beyond yourself— whether they are commitments to religions, to loved ones, to your life's work, to your fellow human beings, or to some conception of an ethical order . . . It leads to questions like, "Why*

am I here? What do I mean in the infinite scheme of things? I could die tomorrow and it wouldn't matter." Call it ego if you like, but you want to count. To count, you must be part of something. Being part of a movement, whether it is labor, business, the environment, civil rights, zoning, or saving whales, is life-giving.

Take a look at the people you know who are role models of vigorous longevity, people filled with joy, rich with friends and excited about their lives until the day they die. We can cite many people: Michelangelo, who painted the Sistine Chapel in his eighties; Paderewski, who still performed at seventy-nine; Helen Keller, who was going strong in her late eighties; and Grandma Moses, who painted until her death at age one hundred and one. All of them demonstrated a strong sense of themselves and their purpose in life. If you find *meaning* in your life, there is no reason you cannot follow their example in your later years.

DEATH—A SUBJECT COMING OUT OF THE CLOSET

There are those who deny that life has any real meaning—because it ultimately ends in death. But those who cultivate an active spiritual life refuse to let their joy and fulfillment be snatched from them by the imminence of death. They live each day to the fullest—a philosophy of living that is a part of most of the world's religions. A Sanskrit proverb expresses it well:

> Look to this day,
> For it is life,
> The very life of life.
> In its brief course lie all
> The realities and verities of existence,
> The bliss of growth,
> The splendor of action
> The glory of power—
>
> For yesterday is but a dream
> And tomorrow is only a vision.

> But today, well lived,
> Makes every yesterday a dream of happiness
> And every tomorrow a vision of hope.

> Look well, therefore, to this day.

Until recently, the subject of death was taboo. Now it has come out of the closet and is the subject of many popular books. *Life after Life* by Raymond Moody gives a convincing argument for the belief suggested by the title. Based on research of people who have been at or near the point of death and then revived, Moody describes their common experiences—and concludes that when the time comes, death is a peaceful and pleasant, rather than unpleasant, experience. Elizabeth Kubler-Ross is perhaps the most widely known expert on the subject. Her best-seller, *On Death and Dying* gives extensive data indicating that death is merely the act of passing to another level of existence. To die is like going through a veil into another reality.

Indeed, the possibility of "easing death" as the alternative to "debilitation, dementia, and dependence, is the next big item on the modern [social] agenda," according to a recent article in *The Economist*. "Modern medicine . . . keeps men and women alive longer than they hoped for even a half a century ago" and often longer than they wish. "The old used to be snatched away by pneumonia, [sometimes called] the old man's friend, or by a heart attack; now pneumonia can be cured with antibiotics and stopped hearts can be [started again.] Man can cheat death."

But if he does, he is likely to suffer the consequences.

Joe Alston, the main character in Wallace Stegner's *The Spectator Bird,* mentioned in Chapter 1, is depressed about his meaningless and unhappy retirement. He has death very much on his mind. He makes a cynical remark about it to his doctor friend, Ben, who responds with, "Death? Death isn't that much of a problem. It's as natural as living, and just as easy, once you've accepted it. I know, because I've been dead twice myself. Both times they revived me."

Fear robs us of contentment, happiness, and peace of mind. Many people entering their third half of life fear growing old and fear dying. But how futile and ridiculous, for *both* are inevitable!

Joe's friend, Ben, made peace with his own mortality, as has author and psychiatrist Scott Peck, who tells us we need to befriend death. He compares it to going into an exam. You need to read and study as much as you can beforehand. Then you won't be afraid when you get there. As in almost every other aspect of the third half of life, *attitude* is everything. William Cullen Bryant perhaps says it best in the magnificent poetry of his classic, "Thanatopsis," which ends with these lines:

> So live, that when thy summons comes to join
> The innumerable caravan, which moves
> To that mysterious realm, where each shall take
> His chamber in the silent halls of death,
> Thou go not, like the quarry-slave at night,
> Scourged to his dungeon, but, sustained and soothed
> By an unfaltering trust, approach thy grave,
> Like one who wraps the drapery of his couch
> About him, and lies down to pleasant dreams.

SPIRITUALITY

The word "spirituality" is used here to embrace several related concepts: an inner feeling of connectedness to a power in the universe that is ultimately good; the sense of a higher purpose and meaning in your life that accompanies this connection and manifests itself in feelings of self-worth, dignity, balance, and well-being; and a basic confidence in life and death.

If you already have this kind of spirituality, nurture it. If not, look for it. You can't *make* it happen to you, but like Rowland Hazard after his meeting with Dr. Jung, and like the millions of members of AA who practice the Twelve Steps, you "till the soil and allow it to grow."

In Jung's *Modern Man in Search of a Soul,* he says, "Reasonableness, sound judgement and science certainly help us over a good part of the road [of life]; yet they do not go beyond that frontier of human life which surrounds the commonplace . . . They afford no answer to the meaning of spiritual suffering. Psychoneurosis must be understood as the suffering of a human being who has not discovered what life means for him . . . Spiritual stagnation causes this state."

Taking a scientific rather than a religious approach, Teilhard de Chardin wrote poetically, "I doubt whether there is a more decisive moment for a thinking being than when the scales fall from his eyes and he discovers that he is not an isolated unit lost in the cosmic solitudes, and realizes that a universal will to live converges in him. In such a vision, a man is seen not as a static center of the world—as he long believed himself to be—but as the leading shoot of evolution, which is something much finer."

READING AND STUDY

One approach to the spiritual search is through the abundance of books and magazine and newspaper articles on the subject. A list of our favorites appears at the end of this book. We urge you, however, to scan any book or article to see if it strikes a chord with *you* before making it your own. Then as you read, highlight the "truths" and insights as you come across them.

Even television recognizes the wide appeal of this subject. For example, author and philosopher Joseph Campbell, in his TV series with Bill Moyers, *The Power of Myth,* showed how the quest for a higher power and meaning in the universe has fascinated man since time began.

EASTERN RELIGIONS

From the East have come Transcendental Meditation (TM), Zen, and Yoga, all techniques to improve one's spiritual condition. Since the 1960s, they have attracted millions of followers, especially among the young, who have made them household words. Each offers techniques that can be helpful to anyone seeking spiritual renewal by stilling the body and mind.

RELIGIOUS COMMUNITIES

Although much of the search for inner meaning takes place in solitude, it is also helpful to be part of a community of people who are on the same journey—a church, synagogue, mosque, or other organized religion. Choose a place where you feel comfortable and are able to be open and honest; it also helps if you find inspiration there. The outer creeds and practices of these religious communities are not what really matters. What does matter is that your experience there brings you closer to God—whatever your concept of God is.

THE ULTIMATE MYSTERY

We offer another quote from Jung in his *Modern Man in Search of a Soul:*

> *During the past thirty years, people from all civilized countries of the earth have consulted me. I have treated many hundreds of patients, the larger number being Protestants; a smaller, Jews; and not more than five or six believing Catholics. Among all my patients in the second half of life, there has not been one whose problem in the last resort was not that of finding a religious outlook on life. It is safe to say that every one of them fell ill because he had lost that which the living religions of every age have given their followers; and none of them has been really healed who did not regain his religious outlook. This of course has nothing whatever to do with the creed or membership of a particular church.*

The Practice of the Presence of God is a remarkable book by "Brother Lawrence," a seventeenth-century French monk. Brother Lawrence had been a soldier and a man-of-the-world. One day, struck by the miracle and beauty of a flowering tree, he was moved to join a Carmelite monastery. In rank he never rose above a kitchen helper. He never wrote anything except some letters. Yet so revolutionary were his ideas and so great his influence that upon his death he was eulogized by the Cardinal of France. That eulogy, together with his observations and philosophy of life as remembered by others, and a meager collection of his letters, were gathered in 1656 into a short book that has endured and helped people for over three centuries.

Brother Lawrence's seminal idea was that God is accessible to anyone and that to live in the presence of God is the central aim of life. Even though he followed the stern routine of prayers and worship services in the monastery, he declared, "I am as close to God in the bustle of the kitchen as in the sanctuary." Writing to a mother superior of a convent, who was ill and troubled about her own lack of faith, he said, "Do not let your prayers distract you from loving

God." Advising another correspondent, he said, "Believe, and count as lost every moment that is not spent in loving God."

Brother Lawrence transcended the trappings of his order and his faith to find a meaning and purpose in life that won him a kind of immortality, if not sainthood.

Polly Berrien Berends, in her book *Coming to Life,* says: "The ability to respond gratefully to problems . . . is one of the first signs of a spiritual awakening. At first we just want to stop the pain. But our pain is teaching us something, bringing us somewhere. Occasionally you meet an individual who, suddenly confined to a wheelchair or facing premature death, expresses gratitude for something his predicament has forced him to see. He tells you how shallow his life was before his accident jolted him. His face is radiant, full of peace, joy, compassion. When he laughs, you hear that he knows something you don't. When you first meet such people, you feel horrified by what they lack, but you leave wondering if you will ever see what they have seen." (Proctor, whose remarkable story was told in chapter 4, is such an individual. You may want to read it again in light of Ms. Berends' insights.)

Ralph Ahlberg says, "God is not a belief. He is an experience . . . God is easier to know than to describe." And from a different approach, Teilhard de Chardin arrives at the same place when he says, "On some given day, a man suddenly becomes conscious that he is alive to a particular perception of the divine spread everywhere around him. Question him, 'When did this state begin for him?' He cannot tell. All he knows is that a new spirit has crossed his life. He has acquired a new quality or a new dimension."

This was apparently the experience of T. Helveg, the physicist who, in 1992, discovered aberrations in radio waves that brought the scientific world closer than it had ever been before to the big bang theory that marked the beginning of the universe. Hailed worldwide, this achievement was called "the greatest advance since Galileo."

In the press conference that followed, Helveg made this startling statement: "The further back we go, the nearer we come to God." Reporters immediately pounced on the words, asking, "Whatever do you mean, Dr. Helveg?" He answered simply, "There is an incredible power and order that we do not understand."

19

Public Policy Issues

The strength of a democracy is not in bureaucracy, it is in the people and their communities . . . Let us unleash the potential of our most precious resource: our citizens themselves . . . That's what America is all about.

—George Bush

We'd be better off for social and economic reasons to allow our senior citizens greater opportunities and incentives to remain in the labor market . . . Eventually government policy will have to be brought in line with the facts of life. People are living longer and healthier lives. There's no reason they can't lead more productive lives as well.

—Michael Boskin, in The Wall Street Journal

Thus far we have focused primarily on *you* as an individual as you approach the third half of your life. However, governmental and economic systems, policies, practices and attitudes also affect your well-being. Unfortunately, policy in both the government and private sectors is lagging behind many of the factors we have considered —the changing perceptions of aging, continuing lifework, financial plans—so we shall address only a few of the most critical areas.

HISTORICAL BACKGROUND

George Bush's words touch on how freedom and self-responsibility are intended to function in a free society. In a democracy, each citizen strives for balance between individualism and community, between self-reliance and teamwork, between competition and cooperation.

In America's early days, when there was minimal government, individual and community affairs were handled privately and locally. In those days, although a few people lived to a ripe old age, the *average* life expectancy was less than forty, mainly because of high mortality rates among infants and children. At that time and throughout the nineteenth century, people expected to be taken care of in their old age by their children, and families relied on private savings for this, because Social Security and pension plans didn't exist.

By the 1930s, although average life expectancy was still only sixty, enough people were living longer that the U.S. government decided sixty-five should be established as the age for mandatory retirement, as it had been in Europe. Social Security legislation was passed and many corporations introduced pension plans. Since the end of World War II, our ever-increasing reliance on these sources of retirement income has bred a kind of "entitlement mentality" in the general population.

The combination of government social legislation, corporate paternalism, and demands of organized labor for pensions and other retirement benefits has weakened the historical sense of self-reliance and has fostered the traditional concept of "retirement" as an endless vacation. The implication is that Social Security, pensions, health insurance, and annuity plans should cover retirees' expenses for the few years they have left. This inclination is psychologically unhealthy and financially impractical.

Obviously, this bleak bill of goods is in direct contrast to the picture we painted in the preceding pages. More importantly, it is inconsistent with today's facts. A child born in 1990 has, on the average, a life expectancy of about seventy-five years; those who reach sixty and are entering their third half can expect to live into their eighties; and those who reach eighty can expect to see ninety. So much for dry statistics. We're convinced that with a positive physical, mental, and spiritual state of being, active and healthy people like those we have repeatedly cited are likely to have twenty to thirty years of productivity ahead of them as they enter their third half of life.

This brings us to the issues that need to be addressed in the public policy arena.

FUTURE WORK FORCE REQUIREMENTS

During the past fifteen years, technological and related organizational changes have reinforced blind adherence to "early out" policies by industrial corporations and businesses. The result has been a serious demobilization of experienced workers and managers. They are being evicted with a destructive dual message. On one hand, the message says, "You are over the hill, a bit too old for today's competitive standards. Go out to the pasture. Relax." On the other hand, they are cautioned, "You will just have enough money from Social Security, pension plans, health insurance and annuities to take reasonably good care of the *nonworking*(!) rest of your life."

This is a short-sighted practice that is bad for the people, bad for the corporations, and bad for society. National data shows that life expectancy for those who leave large corporations for a traditional retirement in total leisure is just three years! And extrapolations of past trends indicate that by the end of the 1990s, the demographics of the workplace will have reversed—there will be too many jobs open and too few available workers below age fifty-five. U.S. business will have digested the current technological revolution, moved into the information age, and will be trying to find workers in order to exploit global opportunities.

FLEXIBILITY IN THE WORKPLACE

The other side of the coin is that there are about three million people (nearly two million men and more than one million women) over sixty-five who are working full time. And another two million would like to be.

Where full-time positions for this age group are not possible, some enlightened companies have developed more flexible arrangements to take advantage of this pool of experience. They hire retirees as temporary employees—"temps"—not only in clerical jobs but in professional capacities, thus avoiding the costly drain of benefits on the permanent payroll. They change employees from full-time to part-time status, with commensurate reduction in salary; such arrangements may take the form of shorter work days or partial work weeks. They may even go to "flex time," allowing the employees to set their own schedules, or work at home.

UNRECOGNIZED PRODUCTIVITY POTENTIAL

"Pushing older workers out becomes almost a tragedy," says Dr. Martin Sicker, director of AARP's Worker Equity Initiative. "We must figure out ways to make better use of [senior] human resources." He points out that older workers are less likely to miss work, are more polite to customers, and are more loyal and emotionally stable.

Recognizing these assets, some companies have formal programs to retain older workers. Outstanding examples are Corning Glass, which has had such a program for twenty years; and Travelers Insurance, with a ten year track record in this area. Other such companies include Polaroid, Xerox, IBM, Grumman, Varian Associates, and Wells Fargo Bank. A few companies have actually targeted older people for their permanent staffs. Examples include Days Inn, Builders Emporium, and Texas Refinery Corporation.

PUNITIVE GOVERNMENT POLICIES, PRACTICES, AND ATTITUDES

The private and public sectors need to adjust their attitudes and policies. Social Security is available at age sixty-two with a discount, and most company pension plans are structured so that the pension doesn't improve much after age sixty. As a result, the average retirement age in the United States is sixty-two.

Between Social Security and Medicare, one-third of federal government outlays go to seniors, a situation that is burdensome to active wage earners still in the work force, and which has led to a portion of Social Security income becoming taxable. It's expected that the rate of growth in the third half population, coupled with escalating health care costs, will soon mean that one-half of federal government outlays will go to seniors.

Once a person is on Social Security, there is a tax *disincentive* to work for pay until he or she reaches seventy. As was pointed out earlier, in 1993, for every $2.00 a person between sixty-two and sixty-five earns above $7,680, $1.00 is deducted from his or her Social Security payment—creating, in effect, a fifty percent tax on this income, in addition to the tax on the $2.00 itself! (Between the ages sixty-five and seventy, $1.00 is deducted for every $3.00 earned above $10,560.) According to The National Center for Policy Analysis, in Dallas, Texas, this blatantly unfair rule could result, in a hypothetical case, in an individual marginal tax rate of 102 percent under the current tax law!

A majority of the 1991–92 U.S. House of Representatives called for the outright repeal of this earnings limitation. But the move was blocked by the House Ways and Means Committee. They apparently calculated the loss of budget revenue only, without attempting to quantify the offsets from the additional economic development that would ensue, plus increased Social Security and federal income taxes on income earned between age sixty-two and seventy.

These issues are being addressed by advocacy groups such as The Commonwealth Fund, the Southport Institute for Policy Analysis, and the AARP Worker Equity Initiative. In particular, the AARP group is assessing the impact of an aging work force on society, and working to:

- eliminate all forms of age discrimination in the workplace;
- improve the image of older workers;
- encourage the creation of job opportunities for older persons;
- help older people make informed decisions about employment and retirement.

All three advocacy groups agree that current private and public policies and legislation not only have a debilitating effect on individual Americans but exert an equally negative influence on society.

STEREOTYPES AND MONEY

Attaining a joyous and fulfilling third half is mostly up to the individual, but individual initiative is hobbled today by negative stereotypes of aging and the public policies that result. The stereotype of older people is that they are poor, sick, doddering, non-working and content to loaf or play shuffleboard until they die. The truth is, today's retirees are better off financially than any preceding generation. Only one in ten is classified as poor; and eight out of ten are "more than marginally self-sufficient." A majority are healthy, fit, and would like to work for pay on some basis. No doubt many would like to try new business ventures or civic and volunteer endeavors.

They could be responsible for funding more of their own financial needs, including health insurance and health care, were it not for the bias against them. The policies of Congress are openly against the accumulation of "wealth" (any excess savings) by individuals; and proliferating government regulation stifles the incentive to start a small business. No wonder there is an "entitlement mentality" among so many!

This cultural conditioning against individual enterprise is harming our economy and our society. As Michael Boskin said, opening this chapter, "Eventually government policy will have to be brought into line with the facts of life. People are leading longer and healthier lives. There's no reason they can't lead more productive lives as well."

RESEARCH ON AGING

The Institute of Medicine in the National Academy of Sciences has issued a report called "Extending Life. Enhancing Life. A National Research Agenda on Aging." This report recommends nearly doubling public and private funding for aging research. It says, "The twentieth century, in which humankind has gained some twenty-five years in average life expectancy, is proof that public health and medical research are winning propositions. Let's continue the trend."

Of fifteen priority areas recommended for study, one concerns "behavioral and social interventions that enhance the quality of life." We hope that in this area, research will support the perceived human need for a continuing lifework, and that this support will lead to public policy developments encouraging the potential for productive and beneficial work by people in the fifty-five to eighty-five age group.

THE RIGHT TO DIE

One vital aspect of individual independence and self-reliance in later years is the right to choose to end one's life when the quality of that life is gone. The ability of the medical profession to prolong "life," even in cases of catastrophic illnesses or injury, has outdistanced the ethical and moral dilemmas involved. "Warehousing" such patients indefinitely—often years or even decades—against the wishes of the victims and their families imposes a frightful economic and emotional cost.

In earlier days, northern Indians migrated between summer hunting grounds and winter camps. When the old and infirm of the tribe no longer were able to cross the river, they were given food and drink and gently, lovingly left on the other side. As heartless as this may seem at first blush, it is downright humane when compared to our current policy of keeping our aged alive, but confined to bed or strapped into wheelchairs, long after their mental faculties and their bodies are gone.

Perhaps more research on aging will help free us from our unthinking dependency on medical bureaucracy and steer us toward more self-reliance regarding the right to die. Recently this subject has come out of the closet and is being discussed and debated in a wide range of community and public forums, including shows such as "60 Minutes." These are hopeful signs.

RETURN TO SELF-RELIANCE?

The unbridled individualism that characterized America's first century has rightfully fallen into disrepute. Perhaps we have forgotten that from the end of the Civil War until the 1930s, individual citizens often joined together for their common good. Among the many mutual aid organizations were churches, secret societies, and fraternal insurance associations. In most parts of the country, particularly urban industrial areas, the great majority of people were privately covered by life, accident, and health insurance policies issued either by commercial companies or mutual aid societies.

During the Great Depression, social welfare legislation by the government and paternalism by big corporations severely weakened these private efforts. The result: a loss of self-reliance and the rise of the "entitlement mentality."

On the positive side, America has always had a cultural conditioning toward philanthropy. People have been glad to give back to the community something of what they have gained through their hard work; and businesses have accepted their social responsibility through corporate giving. This kind of philanthropy is recognized and protected by our tax laws. What's needed now is legislation and cultural conditioning to encourage people in or near their third half stage to pursue a lifework, thus continuing their ability to contribute to society through philanthropic giving and through volunteering their time, efforts, and talents.

❧ 20 ❧

In Conclusion—
A New American Frontier

People who seem to be the happiest and healthiest at any age are those who have a sense of community. These people are connected with others by mutual need, have a sense of identity, know themselves and respect themselves; and they see and work toward a purpose in their lives. They are active, engaged in something that gives them a reason to get out of bed and organize the day.

—Geri Marr Burdman

The concepts that comprise this book testify to the condition described by Geri Burdman in her book *Healthful Aging*. What's next? Before we try to answer, let's take a look at the journey you've made.

To begin with, you saw that a quiet revolution is taking place. Earlier stereotypes of aged people are outmoded and the old model of retirement is being replaced with the perspective that "to rest is to rust." Society is recognizing that the "third half" of life can be long, active, abundant, and fulfilling—particularly if it involves some kind of lifework.

The "silent" generation is picking up the torch of this quiet revolution. Its members were born into a world of different values and have gone through more traumas and survived more crises than any generation in history. But now, in their fifties and sixties, they have good health, a new freedom, and more money than their predecessors. They are pioneers, replacing growing older with "older growing."

(They will be the model for future generations.)

In this they are consistent with recognized theories of evolution and human development as promulgated by Toynbee, Teilhard de Chardin, Jung, Erickson, and Levinson. They refuse to be misled by destructive myths that intelligence and memory decrease with age. By *using* their brains instead of neglecting them, and by adopting new attitudes and a positive "mind-set," they can continue to grow as long as they live.

The most important element is to continue to have a "work" in the third half. People need to feel needed, to be fulfilled and to contribute to the good of the world. And the extra income doesn't hurt, while you live as fully as you wish. In fact, the third half is the time when people are best qualified for leadership, especially in public service.

In Part II, you learned how several people have managed change and successfully made the transition from the "second half" to the third, by combining learning, leisure, and service to others. Using your notebook, you became more clear about who you are by inventorying your values, interests, capabilities and accomplishments.

And you came to a better understanding of your relationships, how to assure good communication with the people in your life, and how you'll need to handle them differently in the third half.

In planning your transition from a work life to a lifework adventure, use the "E" word formula: what you Enjoy doing; where your Expertise lies; what fruits of Experience you have; how to Enquire into what others need, and how to adopt an Entrepreneurial attitude.

With your financial picture in hand, you realize that you can balance learning and leisure with your lifework. You've gained some new angles on third half travel. You also now have the benefit of insights shared through many both successful and unsuccessful case histories, designed to help you decide where you want to live for the next twenty to thirty years. And we fervently hope, we've convinced you to take charge of your health and wellness through appropriate nutrition and exercise.

The world of money was explored from several angles in Part III. You should now be able to make constructive financial decisions to support your lifestyle objectives. And we hope your confidence in your ability to manage your investments was also enhanced.

IN CONCLUSION— A NEW AMERICAN FRONTIER

Now, in Part IV, you have seen how having *meaning* in your life is essential if you are to be joyful, productive, and fulfilled. And you can even face your own mortality with equanimity. Finally, you have been urged to interest yourself in public policy issues that have a bearing on your lifestyle options.

In short, you have taken charge of your life. So what's next?

It is time to ask yourself the penetrating questions about your lifework adventure that were addressed at the end of chapter 9:

- Your personal values, interests, capabilities, and experience— what new projects can you translate them into that would be exciting to you? Could the project include your spouse?
- Your lifetime hobbies or avocational interests—can any of them become a small business?
- What would you really. *love* to do? What really grabs you? Do you have an unfulfilled dream on the backburner, a repressed crusade you'd love to tackle?
- Can you afford it? How would you manage it financially?
- Do you have the temperment? Would it satisfy your social needs?
- Would it involve the need for more education and personal development?

MASLOW'S HIERARCHY

These are questions that typify the quiet revolution in progress. They indicate how the fundamental nature of the over-fifty population in the United States is changing. Abraham Maslow's human potential theories are valuable in understanding this dramatic shift in the culture of the silent generation.

Maslow charted a hierarchy of our basic human needs as follows. As each level is attained, we move onto the next rung of the ladder. (Read from the bottom up.)

5. Self-actualization (full maturity)
4. Esteem for self and others (mutual respect)
3. Love and belonging (trust)
2. Safety and security (hope)
1. Physiological needs (survival)

He termed the first four levels "deficit driven"; the fifth, "fully functioning." Maslow maintained that the human needs of the first four levels must be met in order to reach the fifth and become a fully functioning person. This is where *you are now.* You met your basic material needs long ago, and you realize that mere "things" do not bring happiness and satisfaction. Your motivations in your maturing years are linked to trust and mutual respect.

David B. Wolfe summed up Maslow's findings with these inspiring words:

> *Self-actualization motivations are not directed toward compensating for deficits, as is true of the lower needs levels, but are directed toward increased richness and growth in a life that now has few deficits . . . Inspiration, not hunger, now motivates behavior. Action [that is motivated by] emptiness gives way to action driven by gratitude for a life with a persistent sense of fulfillment. Beauty is everywhere. [One's] emotions abound in good feelings, continuously delivering life's finest ecstasies. And there is a strong desire to share this bounty with others. That desire grows out of the strengthened sense of connectedness that mature people feel toward the rest of existence.*

COMMUNITY

This "strong desire to share this bounty with others" and "connectedness . . . toward the rest of existence" may lead you to choose a lifework of service to the community. Community may mean your city or town, your school district or neighborhood. Or your concerns and perspective may be regional, national, or even international in scope.

This is what Geri Burdman was referring to at the opening of this chapter: You will be "happiest and healthiest" if you "have a sense of community" and if you "are connected with others by mutual need, have a sense of identity . . . and respect" yourself. You will "work toward a purpose in [your life] . . . engaged in something that gives [you] a reason to get out of bed and organize the day."

IN CONCLUSION— A NEW AMERICAN FRONTIER

SELF-RELIANCE AND COOPERATION

The individual self-reliance that we have emphasized here must be balanced with our obligations to society. Bill Moyers spoke eloquently to this paradox in a commencement address at Middlebury College in 1990. He said:

> *If we're going to create a sustainable and livable society . . . we cannot talk about the economics of competition without also talking about the ethic of cooperation. This means recognizing our capacity to make common cause, to create a political culture that nurtures obligation and honors trust . . .*
>
> *The building of this country was a social and not a solitary endeavor . . . We hear a lot of chest-thumping about rugged individuals and the self-made man, but it's been the ethic of cooperation that inspired our best moments and our most enduring institutions. This talent for social cooperation provided a resilient environment for capitalism. Individual initiative succeeded only if it led to systems of mutual support. "Live and let live" wasn't enough. We had to move to "live and help live . . ."*
>
> *Civilization, you see, is a web of cooperation joining people to family, friends, communities, and country, creating in each of us a sense of reliance on the whole, a recognition of the self in companionship with others, sharing a powerful loyalty to the common good . . .*

The third half of life is a time when many people are self-sufficient, self-responsible, and independent. At the same time they are deeply involved with serving the needs of society.

SOME PEOPLE WHO ARE DOING IT

Here are examples from participants in our Third Half of Life Seminars who have succeeded in doing it:

- A man who had done nothing for a year after his retirement is now free-lancing in home remodeling, works part-time for his town's public works department, and volunteers at the local community center.

- A woman has organized, through her church, a lunch program for the homeless in a nearby city.
- A man has become board chairman and key fund-raiser for an inner-city educational institution for abandoned children.
- A lawyer who had planned to leave the law instead negotiated a reduced-time arrangement with her firm so she could volunteer her legal services with the local agency for retarded citizens.
- One man discovered in retirement latent skills working with his hands. His third-half projects include playing the piano regularly, and serving a leadership role in numerous community organizations, including the hospital.
- A telecommunications expert who had reached a plateau in his career was bored and restless—but afraid to "retire." After he and his wife attended the planning seminar, his attitude changed. His self-renewal resulted in his company offering him a challenging international position, which he accepted. He and his wife now enjoy a larger and more rewarding perspective on life.
- A homemaker has come out of "retirement" to reenter her professional counseling career in social work on a part-time basis.
- A man and his wife settled in a country in Europe, where they bought and restored an historic cottage and became active in village affairs.

How different these lives are from the traditional model of retirement, which advocates a life of pointless leisure. Today, people in the third half are opening new frontiers of American activism and becoming a force in solving problems that trouble our country.

ENDLESS POSSIBILITIES

In your third half, you will have time to be altruistic. You possess talents, experience, mature wisdom, and leadership abilities that can be woven into the fabric of society. The possibilities are endless, but we know from our seminars that four areas consistently emerged with particular intensity.

IN CONCLUSION— A NEW AMERICAN FRONTIER

EDUCATION

Nothing is more important to the future of America than better education for our youngsters. Many troubled public schools now welcome volunteer help—or at the very least can steer you toward disadvantaged students who need tutoring. For example, students for whom English is a second language often need help. Literacy tutoring is an area of crying need, and any mature adult who can read can help. Private schools usually do not require a teaching certificate, so your particular expertise may be put to use in any number of ways.

Adult education—often called "continuing education" in community and job-training programs—is usually less traditionally organized than schools. Third-half people can be a major resource. Take actor Eddie Albert, who at eighty-four is operating a school for six hundred latch-key kids. Now there's real commitment!

THE ENVIRONMENT

The environment is a prime concern at every community level: local, regional, national, and global. Environmental deterioration, ecology, conservation of resources, and population control, which are all linked, have become hot issues. They are also areas that welcome dedicated energy and experience, either on a paid or volunteer basis.

A third-half advertising executive is in charge of the recycling program of a medium-sized eastern city. Another easterner, on vacation in the state of Washington, became incensed at the sight of hundreds of square miles of virgin forests denuded by clear-cutting. As a result, he decided to move west upon retirement and become an activist in saving the trees.

Numerous volunteer citizen-action groups can be found in the environmental field; paid work is less visible. One example is the Senior Environment Employment Program (SEEP), established jointly by the Environmental Protection Agency and AARP. SEEP, which is administered by AARP, operates in all ten EPA regions and Washington, D.C. The program uses both highly technical and lay people, either part time or full time; any experienced person over age fifty-five can qualify.

GOVERNANCE

As this book goes to press, most of our major cities, many states, and the federal government are in dire straits. Budgets (and accompanying deficits) are out of control; health care and education have reached the crisis stage; and economic and environmental issues seem to defy formulation of long-term policy. Special interest groups and Political Action Committees subvert the democratic process. (A veteran senator, trying to answer accusations of influence-peddling in the savings and loan scandal, defended himself by saying, "You all know that I did nothing that everyone else does not do.") Bipartisan commissions are appointed to address grave problems, only to have their recommendations ignored!

Many people have expertise and experience in the field of governance. They have contributed to hospital, musuem, or school administration—but the rough-and-tumble world of politics is another matter. Remember what Dag Hammarskjold said: "It is when we play safe that we create a world of utmost insecurity."

You might consider joining one of the urban "leadership" programs that are springing up around America. They work because they bring divergent special interests together to act as a team. An effective example is "Leadership Santa Barbara County" in California.

People in the third half of life constitute the best hope for making government more effective because, in accordance with Maslow's theory, they no longer have to strive and hence, no longer have a "special interest." They are not driven by personal ambition. They don't have to prove themselves to anyone. What they're seeking is to further their personal growth and to have the satisfaction of making the world a better place.

OUR CULTURAL HERITAGE

Many of the silent generation, now entering their third half are assuming responsibility as role models to help restore our eroding cultural heritage. Stephen Knack, in a "New Year's Eve 1990" article in *The Wall Street Journal,* asks: "Why do fewer and fewer of us who are eligible, register and vote? Why are both newspaper reading and TV news ratings down and declining? Why the increased lack of cooperation with the census takers? Why are crime rates up and climbing? Why are more college and university students cheating on examinations? Why are charitable contributions, adjusted for income and tax inducements, trending down? Why is federal income tax compliance falling? Why does this apparent lack of responsibility, honesty, and civic-mindedness seem most prevalent among young adults?"

Knack cites several possible reasons, including increased urban anonymity, less peer pressure, more singles and one-parent families, and more working mothers. To which we might add that Bill Moyers' message is obviously not reaching enough young people! That is, the lessons of American history—which in many ways, is the story of the most effective civilization ever—are not being learned. And role models are either lacking or flawed. Here is an opportunity for people in the third half. Character and leadership must surely come from mature adults who are self-actualized (in Maslow's terms) and willing to face the challenge of becoming role models for the generations that follow.

A REVOLUTION OF THE MIND

In his book, *The Lessons of History,* Will Durant expressed the thought that the only *real* revolution is in the mind. He basically believed that the Renaissance of the 14th and 15th century was the liberation of the mind to believe as it wanted. The quiet revolution could be the cause of another renaissance in the late twentieth century. Because of the magnitude of change involved, it could turn out to be a new spurt in evolution—not a biological evolution, but a social one.

People in their third half of life could be the leaders of this evolution. Durant observed that the one dominant characteristic of history's great leaders was that they had a strong sense of purpose. They were not necessarily "good" people but they had something they strongly believed in that drove them. President Kennedy also believed in the value of history. He felt that great presidents were great precisely because they had a sense of history and a sense of their particular role in it. The same potential and opportunity exist for each of us.

GO FOR IT!

The time has arrived when you must begin to make your decisions about how you will spend the twenty to thirty years of the third half of your life. We encourage you to embrace this next stage with optimism and confidence that you will be blessed with health, wellness, and meaning in your life. Find a lifework that will be fulfilling to you and helpful to the world and we promise you will feel useful and satisfied.

Yes, there *is* a new American frontier—the "third half" of life! And it's waiting for you. You can pioneer new roles in this world. You can break new ground—and in the process, attain a joy and sense of purpose you never dreamed possible. By redefining your retirement, you will reinvent your life.

THIRD HALF OF LIFE
INSTITUTE'S
SEVEN-POINT CHECKLIST

HOW PREPARED—HOW READY—ARE YOU?
. . . TO MANAGE YOUR TRANSITION OUT OF YOUR
FULL-TIME CAREER LIFE INTO THE THIRD HALF
OF YOUR LIFE?

	Mostly	*Partially*	*Not*
1. I am clear about who I am, what motivates me, and what my attitudes are.	—	—	—
· I know my major accomplishments in my worklife, my civic life, my family life.	—	—	—
· I know my primary capabilities—skills, talents, expertise.	—	—	—
· I know my priority interests in the areas of work, learning, and leisure.	—	—	—
· I know the qualities that characterize my behavior.	—	—	—
· I know my prime values and beliefs.	—	—	—
2. Relationships with family, friends, and associates are clearly prioritized.	—	—	—
· I know how I innately take in and process data, and how I reach decisions.	—	—	—
· I know how to listen receptively.	—	—	—
· I know how best to present myself and my ideas.	—	—	—
3. I have prioritized my lifework plans, and I intend to continue to "make a difference."	—	—	—
· I have an entrepreneurial attitude.	—	—	—
· I have an interest in civic leadership.	—	—	—

HOW PREPARED—HOW READY—ARE YOU? *(cont.)*

	Mostly	Partially	Not
· I have an interest in mentoring, teaching, or consulting.	—	—	—
· I have a small business interest.	—	—	—
4. My financial plans are in order.	—	—	—
· I can forecast my annual expenses.	—	—	—
· I can forecast my annual income.	—	—	—
· My assets and investments are allocated to my satisfaction.	—	—	—
· My estate and tax plans are set.	—	—	—
5. My learning and leisure priorities are clear.	—	—	—
· I know how I want to continue my education, formally and/or experientially.	—	—	—
· I know how I want to organize my travels.	—	—	—
· I know which leisure and recreational activities I wish to continue or develop.	—	—	—
6. I have decided where I want to live in order to implement my plans and achieve my goals.	—	—	—
· My relationship priorities will be met.	—	—	—
· My lifework priorities will be met.	—	—	—
· My finances will support my plans.	—	—	—
· My learning priorities will be met.	—	—	—
· My leisure priorities will be met.	—	—	—
7. My commitments to my health and wellness standards are clear.	—	—	—
· I do not smoke.	—	—	—
· I drink moderately, if at all.	—	—	—
· My nutrition standards are being met.	—	—	—
· My exercise standards are being met.	—	—	—

If your check marks show you are mostly prepared, congratulations. If too many of your marks fell in the partially or not ready columns, you have some work to do.

THE THIRD HALF OF LIFE™ SEMINAR©

If you are in your forties, fifties, or sixties and anticipating changes in your career, a change in family responsibilities, including care of parents or going through the throes of divorce or bereavement; if you are nearing the "retirement zone" (fifty-five and beyond) and want to reconsider previous thoughts and plans; or if, for whatever reasons, you would just welcome a chance to get a new view of your life, to stand back from it, to review where you have been, and to create a vision of where you want to go—in a short period of time in the stimulation of other people—the Third Half of Life Seminar was designed for you. It is for anyone contemplating or facing significant changes in their work or personal lives.

Conducted by the Third Half of Life Institute, the seminar is an intensive, practical, and philosophical experience. Over three days, with a small group of peers who are wrestling with the same issues, you privately examine your past and present life as a departure point for your short-term and long-term future. Held in a residential setting, it allows you "time out" to concentrate on your life's dreams and desires. Sessions focus on self-discovery, lifestyle planning, life-work planning, finances, and communications.

During a Third Half of Life Seminar, you explore ways of turning your particular background as well as learning, leisure, and professional experiences into a rewarding and fulfilling mixture for your future years. This is accomplished in a carefully designed workbook of your own, in which you will gather your life and plans together. By this process, you remember how much you have done, how much you have to offer, and how distinctive and unique your life is. Your carefully designed workbook becomes your guidebook and serves as a resource in your ongoing life-planning process in the years to come.

By the end of the three days you will have:

- Begun to see yourself from a new perspective — your accomplishments; your unique experiences; how different and special your life has been; and how it all can contribute to a long, productive, and satisfying life until the day you die;
- mapped out your values, interests, skills, talents, experience, accomplishments, and dreams into a composite "you";
- examined the key elements to be included in your financial planning;
- had a wonderfully rich chance to bounce ideas around with like-minded people;
- looked at ways you can develop as a business, community, and civic leader and provide the community (local, national, international) and our society with the continuing service it needs from experienced people;
- begun identifying people in your network who can provide you with the information you need to forge your future plans;
- developed a strategy for exploring your options and opportunities;
- gone through a process of zeroing in on your prime goal(s), using your favorite capabilities, while identifying what further learning may be in order;
- had practical experience in communicating your value;
- learned how to convert your life experience and interests into a realistic plan;
- learned a methodology through hands-on experience that you can use over and over again throughout your life;
- developed a vision and a plan for how to create a future that excites you; and
- found a basis for establishing your well-being as an adult that will be enhanced by your new vision of who you are and the meaning and purpose of your life.

THE THIRD HALF OF LIFE Ⓣⓜ SEMINAR

Participating in the Third Half of Life Seminar is an especially remarkable learning experience that has made a world of difference to those who have taken it. One past participant described it well when he called it a post-graduate Advanced Management Course for Life.

If you have put many years into working hard to educate your children, this chance to have an important educational experience for yourself is well deserved. Make an investment in yourself and your own life and turn your life experiences into the experience of your lifetime. This will be a time to re-assess your tapped, and untapped, talents and aspirations in the company of peers who will share some of their thoughts and ideas as well as listen to yours.

For more information on the Third Half of Life Seminar, contact Tony Colao, Director of MasterMedia's Speaker's Bureau, at (800) 4-LECTUR.

INFORMATION RESOURCES
FOR YOUR LIFEWORK
ADVENTURE

Listed below are national organizations that provide information and opportunities involving community service, business interests, or civic activities.

Action/VISTA
806 Connecticut Avenue NW
Washington, DC 20525

American Association for
   International Aging
1133 20th Street NW
Washington, DC 20036

American Association of Retired
   Persons
601 E Street NW
Washington, DC 20049

Cathedral College of the Laity
Episcopal Church House
Mount St. Albans
Washington, DC 20016

Center for Entrepreneurial
   Management
311 Main Street
Worcester, MA 01608

CORO Foundation
4219 Laclede Avenue
St. Louis, MO 63108

Global Volunteers
375 East Little Canada
   Road
St. Paul, MN 55117

Habitat for Humanity
   International
21 Habitat Street
Americus, GA 31709

International Executive Service
   Corps
8 Stamford Forum
Stamford, CT 06901

Literacy Volunteers
700 Water Street
Syracuse, NY 13210

INFORMATION RESOURCES

Mature Temps
1759 K Street NW
Washington, DC 20006

National Association of
  Community Leadership
One Jackson Square
233 McCrea Street
Indianapolis, IN 46225

National Center for Citizen
  Involvement
1214 16th Street NW
Washington, DC 20036

National Executive Service Corps
257 Park Avenue South
New York, NY 10010

National Park Service
Department of the Interior
Room 1310
Washington, DC 20240

New Career Opportunities
625 North Maryland Avenue
Glendale, CA 90005

Project 55
20 Nassau Street
Princeton, NJ 08542

Second Careers Program
611 South Oxford Street
Los Angeles, CA 90005

Service Corps of Retired
  Executives
Small Business Administration
1441 L Street NW
Washington, DC 20416

VIE c/o Association of Junior
  Leagues
825 Third Avenue
New York, NY 10022

Work in America Institute
700 White Plains Road
Scarsdale, NY 10583

BIBLIOGRAPHY FOR
MAKING IT HAPPEN

The philosophies and perspectives we've shared in *Beating the Age Game* have been touched on by thousands of other books and articles. Here are some of our favorites.

PART I/ THE NEW PERSPECTIVE

New Perspective

Baker, Russell. *Growing Up.* (Congdon & Weed, NY, 1982)
———. *Good Times.* (Morrow, NY, 1987)
Benson, Herbert. *Your Maximum Mind.* (Random House, NY, 1987)
Brown, David. *Brown's Guide to Growing Gray.* (Delacourte, NY, 1987)
Butler, Robert N. *Why Survive? Being Old in America.* (Harper, NY, 1975)
Butler & Gleason. *Productive Aging/Enhancing Vitality in Old Age.* (Spring, NY, 1985)
Buzan, Tony. *Use Both Sides of Your Brain.* (British Broadcasting Corp., London, 1974)
Durant, Will. *The Story of Civilization.* (Simon & Schuster, NY, 1935)
———. *The Lessons of History.* (Simon & Schuster, NY, 1968)
Dychtwald, Kenneth. *Age Wave.* (Bantam, NY, 1990)
Erikson, Erik. *Identity and the Life Cycle.* (Norton, NY, 1980)
Gould, Robert. *Transformations.* (Simon & Schuster, NY, 1978)
Greenleaf, Robert. *The Servant as Leader.* (Greenleaf Center, Newton, MA, 1970)

BIBLIOGRAPHY FOR MAKING IT HAPPEN

Hendrix, Harville. *Getting All the Love You Want.* (Harper, NY, 1988)

Jung, C. G. *Memories, Dreams and Reflections.* (Random House, NY, 1961)

———. *The Undiscovered Self.* (Little Brown, Boston, MA, 1957)

Kelsey, Morton. *Myth, Faith and History.* (Paulist Press, NY, 1979)

LeShan, Eda. *The Wonderful Crisis of Middle Age.* (Knopf, NY 1951)

Levinson, Daniel. *The Seasons of a Man's Life.* (Knopf, NY, 1978)

Peck, Scott. *The Road Less Traveled.* (Touchstone, NY, 1978)

Russell, Peter. *The Brain Book.* (Routledge & Kegan, London, 1979)

Sheehy, Gail. *Passages.* (Dutton, NY, 1976)

Teilhard de Chardin. *The Phenomenon of Man.* (Harper, NY, 1959)

Toynbee, Arnold. *A Study of History.* (Random House, NY, 1970)

Career/Lifework

Bardwick, Judith. *The Plateauing Trap.* (American Management Association, NY, 1986)

Bolles, Richard. *The Three Boxes of Life.* (Ten Speed, Berkeley, CA, 1978)

———. *What Color Is Your Parachute.* (Ten Speed, Berkeley, CA, 1992)

Burton and Wedemeyer. *In Transition.* (Harper, NY, 1991)

Creedy, Richard. *Time Is Money.* (Dutton, NY, 1980)

Drucker, Peter. *The Age of Discontinuity.* (Harper, NY, 1968)

Handy, Charles. *The Age of Unreason.* (Harvard Business School Press, Boston, 1990)

Jackson, Tom. *The Perfect Resumé.* (Doubleday, NY, 1981)

Jackson, Tom and Ellen. *Perfect Resumé Strategies.* (Doubleday, NY, 1992)

Naisbitt, John. *Megatrends.* (Warner, NY, 1990)

Raynolds, John and Eleanor. *Beyond Success.* (MasterMedia, NY, 1988)

Sturman, Gerald. *If You Knew Who You Were . . . You Could Be Who You Are!* (Bierman House, Woodstock, NY, 1989)

———. *Managing Your Career with "Power."* (Bierman House, Greenwich, CT, 1990)

Syms, Marcy. *Mind Your Own Business.* (MasterMedia, NY, 1992)

Toffler, Alvin. *Power Shift.* (Bantam, NY, 1990)

PART II/ HOW TO MAKE IT HAPPEN

Health and Wellness

The American Medical Association Encyclopedia of Medicine. (Random House, NY, 1989)

BIBLIOGRAPHY FOR MAKING IT HAPPEN

Adams, Fisher, and Yanowitz. *An Owner's Manual for the Human Body.* (Vitality House International, 1991)

Benson, Herbert. *The Relaxation Response.* (Morrow, NY, 1975)

Claessens, Sharon. *The Lose Weight Naturally Cookbook.* (Rodale, Emmaus, PA, 1985)

Cousins, Norman. *Anatomy of an Illness.* (Norton, NY, 1979)

Fifty Simple Things You Can Do to Save Your Life. (Earth Works, Berkeley, CA, 1992)

Fredericks, Carlton. *Arthritis: Don't Learn to Live with It.* (Putnam, NY, 1981)

Hensel, Bruce. *Smart Medicine: How to Get the Most Out of Your Medical Checkup and Stay Healthy.* (Putnam, NY, 1989)

The Johns Hopkins Medical Handbook. (Rebus, NY, 1992)

Louria, Donald. *Your Healthy Body, Your Healthy Life: How to Take Control of Your Medical Destiny.* (MasterMedia, NY, 1989)

The Mayo Clinic Family Health Book. (Morrow, NY, 1990)

Pelletier, Kenneth. *Mind as Healer, Mind as Slayer.* (Dell, NY, 1977)

Ryan and Travis. *The Wellness Workbook.* (Ten Speed, Berkeley, CA 1986)

Sanford, Jack. *Healing and Wholeness.* (Paulist Press, NY, 1977)

Siegel, Bernie S. *Love, Medicine and Miracles.* (Harper, NY, 1986)

———. *Peace, Love and Healing.* (Harper, NY, 1989)

Weight Watcher's Favorite Recipes. (Plume, NY, 1986)

Wilson, Jane. *Eating Well When You Just Can't Eat the Way You Used To.* (Workman, NY, 1987)

Witkin, Georgia. *The Female Stress Syndrome.* (Newmarket Press, 1991)

General

Brazelton, Terry. *To Listen to a Child.* (Addison-Wesley, Reading, MA, 1984)

Brown, Jackson. *Life's Little Instruction Book.* (Rutledge Hill, Nashville, TN, 1991)

Coulson, Robert. *Fighting Fair.* (Free Press, MacMillan, NY, 1983)

Fisher, Roger. *Getting to Yes.* (Houghton Mifflin, Boston, 1981)

Gardner, John. *Self Renewal.* (Harper, NY, 1965)

Johnson, Robert. *He.* (Harper, NY, 1974)

———. *She.* (Harper, NY, 1977)

Keirsey and Bates. *Please Understand Me.* (Prometheus Nemesis Books, Del Mar, CA, 1978)

Lee, Alice and Fred. *A Field Guide to Retirement.* (Doubleday, NY 1991)

BIBLIOGRAPHY FOR MAKING IT HAPPEN

Lindbergh, Anne Morrow. *Gift from the Sea.* (Random House, NY, 1955)

Tannen, Deborah. *You Just Don't Understand.* (Morrow, NY 1990)

PART III/ YOUR MONEY

Buchanan, E. W. *Estate Planning, Wills, and Trusts.* (Beverly Farms, MA, 1989)

Dun & Bradstreet. *Guide to Your Investment $.* (Harper, NY, 1992)

Esperti and Peterson. *Loving Trust.* (Viking, NY, 1988)

Madigan and Kasoff. *The First-Time Investor.* (Prentice-Hall, NY, 1986)

Malkiel, Burton. *A Random Walk Down Wall Street.* (Norton, NY, 1990)

The Attorney's One Hour Guide to Personal Finance and Investments. (Hunter Lewis Associates, Washington, DC, 1992)

PART IV/ A CHANGING AMERICA

Meaning in Your Life

Campbell, Joseph. *The Hero With a Thousand Faces.* (Bollingen Foundation, NY, 1949)

———. *The Power of Myth.* (Doubleday, NY, 1988)

The Course in Miracles. (Freeperson Press, San Francisco, 1975)

Cousins, Norman. *The Words of Albert Schweitzer.* (Newmarket Press, NY, 1984)

Frankl, Victor. *Man's Search for Meaning.* (Washington Square Press, NY, 1963)

Heard, Gerald. *Preface to Prayer.* (Harper, NY, 1944)

Johnston, William. *The Inner Eye of Love.* (Harper, NY, 1968)

Kelly, Thomas. *A Testament of Devotion.* (Harper, NY, 1941)

Kubler-Ross, Elizabeth. *On Death and Dying.* (MacMillan, NY, 1969)

Martin, P.W. *Experiment in Depth.* (Routledge & Kegan, London, 1955)

Maslow, Abraham. *Motivation and Personality.* (Harper, NY, 1970)

Moody, Raymond, Jr. *Life after Life.* (Bantam Books, NY, 1975)

Nouwen, Henri. *The Wounded Healer.* (Doubleday, NY, 1972)

Ring, Kenneth. *Life at Death.* (Coward, McCann & Geoghegan, NY, 1980)

Sanford, Jack. *The Kingdom Within.* (Paulist Press, NY, 1970)

Sheehy, Gail. *Pathfinders.* (Morrow, NY, 1981)

Suzuki, D.T. *Zen Mind, Beginner Mind.* (John Weatherhill, NY, 1970)

Tillich, Paul. *The Eternal Now.* (Scribner, NY, 1963)
Twenty-four Hours a Day. (Hazelden Press, Center City, MI, 1975)
Yogananda, Paramahansa. *Autobiography of a Yogi.* (Self Realization
Fellowship, Los Angeles, 1959)

INDEX

INDEX

ABOUT THE AUTHORS

As a young couple, Jack and Phoebe Ballard became convinced that growing old was no way to live after they witnessed the debilitating impact retirement seemed to have on their parents' generation.

So they began a self-styled study of Eastern and Western philosophy and religion. Their search for answers eventually led them to create their "Third Half of Life Seminar" as a way to teach others that retirement isn't simply the end of a career, but the beginning of a new stage in life—a time that can be rich with new opportunities to learn, grow, and be fulfilled.

Now in their sixties, the Ballards have devoted themselves to a consulting practice specializing in life planning. In particular, they teach that proper preparation during the second half of life—the thirties and forties—can effectively create a "third half"—the time between ages fifty-five and eighty. Most important, that third half could prove to be the best years of a person's life.

Jack Ballard spent thirty years in a successful international career in finance and human resources. Phoebe Ballard, a student of psychotherapy, has spent ten years programming a center for humanistic studies.

The Ballards live in Connecticut, where they are active in their community and serve as leaders of several local organizations.

Additional copies of *Beating the Age Game* may be ordered for $12.95, plus postage and handling: send $2 for the first copy; $1 for each additional copy. Send a check to:

MasterMedia Limited
17 East 89th Street
New York, NY 10128
(212) 260-5600
(800) 334-8232
fax: (212) 546-7638

Jack and Phoebe Ballard are available for speeches and seminars. Please contact MasterMedia's Speakers' Bureau for availability and fee arrangements. Call Tony Colao at (800) 4-LECTUR, or fax: (908) 359-1647.

OTHER MASTERMEDIA
BOOKS

To order MasterMedia books, go to your local bookstore or call (800) 334-8232.

THE PREGNANCY AND MOTHERHOOD DIARY: Planning the First Year of Your Second Career, by Susan Schiffer Stautberg, is the first and only undated appointment diary that shows how to manage pregnancy and career. ($12.95 spiral-bound)

CITIES OF OPPORTUNITY: Finding the Best Place to Work, Live and Prosper in the 1990's and Beyond, by Dr. John Tepper Marlin, explores the job and living options for the next decade and into the next century. This consumer guide and handbook, written by one of the world's experts on cities, selects and features forty-six American cities and metropolitan areas. ($13.95 paper, $24.95 cloth)

THE DOLLARS AND SENSE OF DIVORCE, by Dr. Judith Briles, is the first book to combine practical tips on overcoming the legal hurdles by planning finances before, during, and after divorce. ($10.95 paper)

OUT THE ORGANIZATION: New Career Opportunities for the 1990s, by Robert and Madeleine Swain, is written for the millions of Americans whose jobs are no longer safe, whose companies are not loyal, and who face futures of uncertainty. It gives advice on finding a new job or starting your own business. ($12.95 paper)

AGING PARENTS AND YOU: A Complete Handbook to Help You Help Your Elders Maintain a Healthy, Productive and Independent Life, by Eugenia Anderson-Ellis, is a complete guide to providing care to aging relatives. It gives practical advice and resources to the adults who are helping their elders lead productive and independent lives. Revised and updated. ($9.95 paper)

CRITICISM IN YOUR LIFE: How to Give It, How to Take It, How to Make It Work for You, by Dr. Deborah Bright, offers practical advice, in an upbeat, readable, and realistic fashion, for turning criticism into control. Charts and diagrams guide the reader into managing criticism from bosses, spouses, children, friends, neighbors, in-laws, and business relations. ($17.95 cloth)

BEYOND SUCCESS: How Volunteer Service Can Help You Begin Making a Life Instead of Just a Living, by John F. Reynolds III and Eleanor Raynolds, C.B.E., is a unique how-to book targeted at business and professional people considering volunteer work, senior citizens who wish to fill leisure time meaningfully, and students trying out various career options. The book is filled with interviews with celebrities, CEOs, and average citizens who talk about the benefits of service work. ($19.95 cloth)

MANAGING IT ALL: Time-Saving Ideas for Career, Family, Relationships, and Self, by Beverly Benz Treuille and Susan Schiffer Stautberg, is written for women who are juggling careers and families. Over two hundred career women (ranging from a TV anchorwoman to an investment banker) were interviewed. The book contains many humorous anecdotes on saving time and improving the quality of life for self and family. ($9.95 paper)

YOUR HEALTHY BODY, YOUR HEALTHY LIFE: How to Take Control of Your Medical Destiny, by Donald B. Louria, M.D., provides precise advice and strategies that will help you to live a long and healthy life. Learn also about nutrition, exercise, vitamins, and medication, as well as how to control risk factors for major diseases. Revised and updated. ($12.95 paper)

THE CONFIDENCE FACTOR: How Self-Esteem Can Change Your Life, by Dr. Judith Briles, is based on a nationwide survey of six thousand men and women. Briles explores why women so often feel a lack of self-confidence and have a poor opinion of themselves. She offers step-by-step advice on becoming the person you want to be. ($9.95 paper, $18.95 cloth)

THE SOLUTION TO POLLUTION: 101 Things You Can Do to Clean Up Your Environment, by Laurence Sombke, offers step-by-step techniques on how to conserve more energy, start a recycling center, choose biodegradable products, and even proceed with individual environmental cleanup projects. ($7.95 paper)

OTHER MASTERMEDIA BOOKS

TAKING CONTROL OF YOUR LIFE: The Secrets of Successful Enterprising Women, by Gail Blanke and Kathleen Walas, is based on the authors' professional experience with Avon Products' Women of Enterprise Awards, given each year to outstanding women entrepreneurs. The authors offer a specific plan to help you gain control over your life, and include business tips and quizzes as well as beauty and lifestyle information. ($17.95 cloth)

SIDE-BY-SIDE STRATEGIES: How Two-Career Couples Can Thrive in the Nineties, by Jane Hershey Cuozzo and S. Diane Graham, describes how two-career couples can learn the difference between competing with a spouse and becoming a supportive power partner. Published in hardcover as *Power Partners.* ($10.95 paper, $19.95 cloth)

DARE TO CONFRONT! How to Intervene When Someone You Care About Has an Alcohol or Drug Problem, by Bob Wright and Deborah George Wright, shows the reader how to use the step-by-step methods of professional interventionists to motivate drug-dependent people to accept the help they need. ($17.95 cloth)

WORK WITH ME! How to Make the Most of Office Support Staff, by Betsy Lazary, shows you how to find, train, and nurture the "perfect" assistant and how to best utilize your support staff professionals. ($9.95 paper)

MANN FOR ALL SEASONS: Wit and Wisdom from The Washington Post's *Judy Mann,* by Judy Mann, shows the columnist at her best as she writes about women, families, and the impact and politics of the women's revolution. ($9.95 paper, $19.95 cloth)

THE SOLUTION TO POLLUTION IN THE WORKPLACE, by Laurence Sombke, Terry M. Robertson and Elliot M. Kaplan, supplies employees with everything they need to know about cleaning up their workspace, including recycling, using energy efficiently, conserving water and buying recycled products and nontoxic supplies. ($9.95 paper)

THE ENVIRONMENTAL GARDENER: The Solution to Pollution for Lawns and Gardens, by Laurence Sombke, focuses on what each of us can do to protect our endangered plant life. A practical sourcebook and shopping guide. ($8.95 paper)

THE LOYALTY FACTOR: Building Trust in Today's Workplace, by Carol Kinsey Goman, Ph.D., offers techniques for restoring commitment and loyalty in the workplace. ($9.95 paper)

OTHER MASTERMEDIA BOOKS

DARE TO CHANGE YOUR JOB—AND YOUR LIFE, by Carole Kanchier, Ph.D., provides a look at career growth and development throughout the life cycle. ($9.95 paper)

MISS AMERICA: In Pursuit of the Crown, by Ann-Marie Bivans, is an authorized guidebook to the Pageant, containing eyewitness accounts, complete historical data, and a realistic look at the trials and triumphs of the potential Miss Americas. ($19.95 paper, $27.50 cloth)

POSITIVELY OUTRAGEOUS SERVICE: New and Easy Ways to Win Customers for Life, by T. Scott Gross, identifies what the consumers of the nineties really want and how businesses can develop effective marketing strategies to answer those needs. ($14.95 paper)

BREATHING SPACE: Living and Working at a Comfortable Pace in a Sped-Up Society, by Jeff Davidson, helps readers to handle information and activity overload, and gain greater control over their lives. ($10.95 paper)

TWENTYSOMETHING: Managing and Motivating Today's New Work Force, by Lawrence J. Bradford, Ph.D., and Claire Raines, M.A., examines the work orientation of the younger generation, offering managers in businesses of all kinds a practical guide to better understand and supervise their young employees. ($22.95 cloth)

REAL LIFE 101: The Graduate's Guide to Survival, by Susan Kleinman, supplies welcome advice to those facing "real life" for the first time, focusing on work, money, health, and how to deal with freedom and responsibility. ($9.95 paper)

BALANCING ACTS! Juggling Love, Work, Family, and Recreation, by Susan Schiffer Stautberg and Marcia L. Worthing, provides strategies to achieve a balanced life by reordering priorities and setting realistic goals. ($12.95 paper)

REAL BEAUTY . . . REAL WOMEN: A Handbook for Making the Best of Your Own Good Looks, by Kathleen Walas, International Beauty and Fashion Director of Avon Products, offers expert advice on beauty and fashion to women of all ages and ethnic backgrounds. ($19.50 paper)

THE LIVING HEART BRAND NAME SHOPPER'S GUIDE, (Revised and Updated) by Michael E. DeBakey, M.D., Antonio M. Gotto, Jr., M.D., D.Phil., Lynne W. Scott, M.A., R.D./L.D., and John P. Foreyt, Ph.D., lists brand-name supermarket products that are low in fat, saturated fatty acids, and cholesterol. ($14.95 paper)

OTHER MASTERMEDIA BOOKS

MANAGING YOUR CHILD'S DIABETES, by Robert Wood Johnson IV, Sale Johnson, Casey Johnson, and Susan Kleinman, brings help to families trying to understand diabetes and control its effects. ($10.95 paper)

STEP FORWARD: Sexual Harassment in the Workplace, What You Need to Know, by Susan L. Webb, presents the facts for dealing with sexual harassment on the job. ($9.95 paper)

A TEEN'S GUIDE TO BUSINESS: The Secrets to a Successful Enterprise, by Linda Menzies, Oren S. Jenkins, and Rickell R. Fisher, provides solid information about starting your own business or working for one. ($7.95 paper)

GLORIOUS ROOTS: Recipes for Healthy, Tasty Vegetables, by Laurence Sombke, celebrates the taste, texture, and versatility of root vegetables. Contains recipes for appetizers, soups, stews, and baked, broiled, and stir-fried dishes—even desserts. ($12.95 paper)

THE OUTDOOR WOMAN: A Handbook to Adventure, by Patricia Hubbard and Stan Wass, details the lives of adventurous outdoor women and offers their ideas on how you can incorporate exciting outdoor experiences into your life. ($14.95 paper)

FLIGHT PLAN FOR LIVING: The Art of Self-Encouragement, by Patrick O'Dooley, is a life guide organized like a pilot's flight checklist, which ensures you'll be flying "clear on top" throughout your life. ($17.95 cloth)

HOW TO GET WHAT YOU WANT FROM ALMOST ANYBODY, by T. Scott Gross, shows how to get great service, negotiate better prices, and always get what you pay for. ($9.95 paper)

FINANCIAL SAVVY FOR WOMEN: A Money Book for Women of All Ages, by Dr. Judith Briles, divides a woman's monetary lifespan into six phases, discusses the specific areas to be addressed at each stage, and demonstrates how to create a sound lifelong money game plan. ($14.95 paper)

TEAMBUILT: Making Teamwork Work, by Mark Sanborn, teaches business how to improve productivity, without increasing resources or expenses, by building teamwork among employers. ($19.95 cloth)

THE BIG APPLE BUSINESS AND PLEASURE GUIDE: 501 Ways to Work Smarter, Play Harder, and Live Better in New York City, by Muriel Siebert and Susan Kleinman, offers visitors and New Yorkers alike advice on how to do business in the city as well as how to enjoy its attractions. ($9.95 paper)

MIND YOUR OWN BUSINESS: And Keep It in the Family, by Marcy Syms, COO of Syms Corporation, is an effective guide for any organization, small or large, facing what is documented to be the toughest step in managing a family business—making the transition to the new generation. ($18.95 cloth)

KIDS WHO MAKE A DIFFERENCE, by Joyce M. Roché and Marie Rodriguez, with Phyllis Schneider, is a surprising and inspiring document of some of today's toughest challenges being met—by teenagers and kids! Their courage and creativity allowed them to find practical solutions. ($8.95 paper; with photos)

ROSEY GRIER'S ALL-AMERICAN HEROS: Multicultural Success Stories, by Roosevelt "Rosey" Grier, is a wonderful collection of personal histories, told in their own words by prominent African-Americans, Latins, Asians, and native Americans; each tells of the people in their lives and choices they made in achieving public acclaim and personal success. ($9.95 paper; with photos)

OFFICE BIOLOGY: Why Tuesday Is the Most Productive Day and Other Relevant Facts for Survival in the Workplace, by Edith Weiner and Arnold Brown, teaches how in the '90s and beyond we will be expected to work smarter, take better control of our health, adapt to advancing technology, and improve our lives in ways that are not too costly or resource-intensive. ($21.95 cloth)

ON TARGET: Enhance Your Life and Ensure Your Success, by Jeri Sedlar and Rick Miners, is a neatly woven tapestry of insights on career and life issues gathered from audiences across the country. This feedback has been crystalized into a highly readable guidebook for exploring who you are and how to go about getting what you want from your career and your life. ($11.95 paper)

SOMEONE ELSE'S SON, by Alan A. Winter, explores the parent-child bond in a contemporary story of lost identities, family secrets, and relationships gone awry. Eighteen years after bringing their first son home from the hospital, Trish and Brad Hunter discover they are not his natural parents. Torn between their love for their son, Phillip, and the question of whether they should help him search for his biological parents, the couple must also struggle with the issue of their own biological son. Who is he—and do his parents know their baby was switched at birth? ($18.95 cloth)

OTHER MASTERMEDIA BOOKS

STRAIGHT TALK ON WOMEN'S HEALTH: How to Get the Health Care You Deserve, by Janice Teal, Ph.D., and Phyllis Schneider, is destined to become a health-care "bible" for women concerned about their bodies and their future health. Well-researched, but devoid of confusing medical jargon, this handbook offers access to a wealth of resources, with a bibliography of health-related books and contact lists of organizations, healthlines, and women's medical centers. ($14.95 paper)

THE STEPPARENT CHALLENGE: A Primer for Making it Work, by Stephen J. Williams, Ph.D., shares firsthand experience and insights into the many aspects of dealing with step relationships—from financial issues to lifestyle changes to differences in race or religion that affect the whole family. Peppered with personal accounts and useful tips, this volume is must reading for anyone who is a stepparent, about to become one, or planning to bring children to a second or subsequent marriage. ($13.95 paper)

PAIN RELIEF! How to Say No to Acute, Chronic, and Cancer Pain, by Dr. Jane Cowles, offers a step-by-step plan for assessing pain and communicating it to your doctor, and explains the importance of having a pain plan before undergoing any medical or surgical treatment. This landmark book includes "The Pain Patient's Bill of Rights," and a reusable pain assessment chart designed to help patients and their families make informed decisions. ($22.95 cloth)

MAKING YOUR DREAMS COME TRUE: A Plan For Easily Discovering and Achieving the Life You Want, by Marcia Wieder, introduces an easy, unique, and practical technique for defining, pursuing, and realizing your career and life interests. Filled with stories of real people and helpful exercises, plus a personal workbook, this clever volume will teach you how to make your dreams come true—any time you choose. ($9.95 paper)

WHAT KIDS LIKE TO DO, by Edward Stautberg, Gail Wubbenhorst, Atiya Easterling, and Phyllis Schneider, is a handy guidebook for parents, grandparents, and babysitters who are searching for activities that kids *really* enjoy. Written by kids for kids, this easy-to-read, generously illustrated primer can teach families how to make every day more fun. ($7.95 paper)